Dryburgh Abbey

Dryburgh Abbey

Richard Fawcett and Richard Oram

TEMPUS

First published 2005

Tempus Publishing Limited
The Mill, Brimscombe Port,
Stroud, Gloucestershire, GL5 2QG
www.tempus-publishing.com

British Library Cataloguing in Publication Data.
A catalogue record for this book is available from the British Library.

ISBN 0 7524 3439 X

Typesetting and origination by Tempus Publishing Limited
Printed in Great Britain

Contents

Preface

This book has been put together in an attempt to provide an illustrated account of the history and architecture of Dryburgh Abbey for those who are looking for something more than could be provided in either a guide book or an on-site display. It must be stressed, however, that there is no intention of offering anything that might be seen as a definitive interpretation; indeed, our understanding of the abbey is not yet at a stage where that could be attempted.

It is hoped that it will be one of a series of occasional publications on major monuments in state care. As with an earlier volume on Melrose Abbey, the authorship has been divided between Richard Oram, who wrote the sections on the history and estates, and Richard Fawcett, who contributed the section on the architecture. It is the authors' hope that their book will make it possible for visitors to derive greater enjoyment from what is generally accepted to be a particularly delightful group of medieval buildings.

Acknowledgements

In writing the architectural section of this book, Richard Fawcett particularly wishes to thank Sue Fawcett and Allan Rutherford for their care in reading through and commenting on earlier drafts of the text. He also wishes to thank David Breeze for his support in the project, Sylvia Stevenson for drawing up the plans and maps, and Mike Brooks, David Henrie and Ailsa MacTaggart for their help with photographic matters.

I

The history of the abbey

INTRODUCTION

Although the ruins of Dryburgh Abbey are amongst the best-known and most substantial of all of Scotland's medieval monasteries, its history is less well understood and far more fragmentary than the physical remains. In large part, this is because, unlike at nearby Melrose Abbey, no member of the monastic community at Dryburgh kept a record of events in their abbey's history, or at least no such chronicle record has survived. Instead, we are reliant on a few very general comments noted down about Dryburgh in chronicles composed elsewhere, Melrose in particular. Sadly, these note only the major events – date of foundation, arrival of the first colony, and so forth – and do not permit us to see the processes by which the community grew and evolved; how it acquired its landed estate; and the various trials, tribulations and triumphs which it confronted and overcame. Instead, we are forced to turn to other forms of documentary source, principally charters, records of rentals of the abbey's estate, and letters and other correspondence concerning its affairs. Here, too, Dryburgh is less fortunate than its neighbours at Kelso and Melrose, in the level of existing documentation from which to recover details of its development over the centuries. What we do have is a fifteenth-century charter book into which the abbey's earlier records were copied, most of them unfortunately without the lists of witnesses from which historians can normally fix at least approximate dates at which they were issued.[1] Even this is an incomplete record, however, for the cartulary – the book into which the early charters were copied – has been damaged, losing its first few folio leaves and an unknown number of pages from its end, with the last charter within it, dating from the late 1330s, breaking off part way through. Later material does exist which allows us to fill in some of the gaps, preserved mainly in later fourteenth- and sixteenth-century royal records or in the cartularies of other monasteries with which Dryburgh had business or legal dealings, plus some stray individual items preserved in private archives, but there are still some very frustrating holes, mainly in the late fourteenth and fifteenth centuries. Nevertheless, it needs to be remembered that there are over

400 surviving, published, documents available concerning Dryburgh, and from them it is possible to construct a richly-textured history of the abbey.

FOUNDATION – THE PREMONSTRATENSIAN ORDER

Amongst the documents lost with the first few pages of the cartulary is the foundation charter issued to the canons by the abbey's founder. This charter would have recorded the reasons for the abbey's foundation and set out the endowment given for its support.[2] With it, we also lost the definitive statement of the identity of the founder and for long, despite the clear assertion of the chronicler based in nearby Melrose Abbey who recorded Dryburgh's foundation by Hugh de Morville, constable of the king of Scots,[3] it was suggested that the abbey was another product of that most prolific of monastic patrons, King David I of Scotland (1124-53).[4] Hugh may have founded the abbey jointly with his wife, Beatrice de Beauchamp, but she is never described in such terms in any of the surviving documents. Instead, she seems to have been an enthusiastic supporter of her husband's project and a generous benefactress to the canons from the start.[5]

Why Hugh was moved to found his abbey remains a mystery, and there is no sign in what we can reconstruct about his life and career to indicate that he was a particularly pious man. There is, surprisingly, no evidence for his active support of any of the major monastic foundations made by his royal master. It is possible that he founded his abbey in emulation of his royal master, or as a proud declaration of his family's arrival in the upper rank of the new nobility which King David was planting in southern Scotland, but such vainglorious motives sit awkwardly with the prevailing spirit of the times. He lived in an age of religious revival, a time of reformation in the Church that was as profound as the better-known Protestant Reformation of the sixteenth century. It was the spirit of evangelical zeal of the time, more than any cynical political or economic motive, which moved David I to support the reform of the Church in his kingdom and to introduce reform-minded monks and canons to carry through the process. It was a period of intense spiritual experience in which laymen were confronted with the sinfulness of their world, shown the deficiencies in their own religious behaviour, and confronted with the likely fate of not only their souls, but also the souls of their families, predecessors and successors. To secure salvation in the hereafter, they were encouraged to give whatever practical aid that they could to the cause of spiritual regeneration. Hugh, who had led an active military career in support of his king's political ambitions,[6] and who had been involved in campaigns which had seen indiscriminate slaughter of civilian populations, attacks on churches and monasteries, and the regular breaking of oaths sworn on holy relics or sponsored by Church authorities, may have felt that only some act of special generosity could save his soul from eternity in hellfire and damnation.

The order which Hugh de Morville chose to colonise his new foundation was not one which had previously enjoyed noble or royal patronage in twelfth-century Scotland. This fact seems to tell against his foundation being done in emulation of David, pointing instead to deeper, personal spiritual reason, and the choice appears to have been a purely personal one on Hugh's part. The Premonstratensian order had itself been founded only in 1120 by St Norbert of Xanten or Genepp, a German nobleman who had abandoned the secular life and become a canon in the cathedral of Xanten. Norbert proved to be one of the most influential spiritual figures of the early 1100s, an able and inspiring preacher who burned with missionary zeal. He sought at first to reform the lifestyle of his fellow canons at Xanten, bidding them to follow the apostolic life, but this radical call was greeted unenthusiastically and Norbert instead left Germany to seek papal permission to preach. In 1119, on the advice of Pope Calixtus II, he came to the diocese of Laon in northern France, where Bishop Bartholomew was engaged in the reform of his see. There, Norbert based himself at Prémontré (from the Latin name for which, *Praemonstratum*, the order subsequently took its name) in the Forêt de St Gobain, west of Laon (*1*). His preaching quickly began to attract followers and before long Bishop Bartholomew was encouraging the reluctant Norbert to form them into an order.

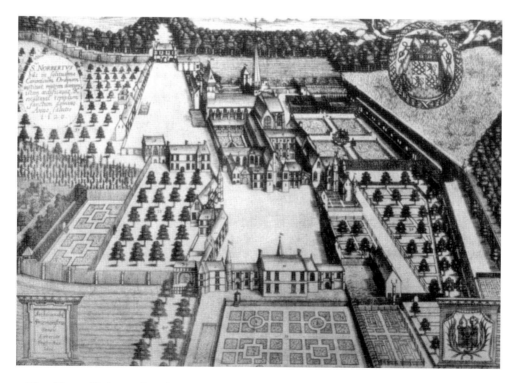

1 The abbey of Prémontré, as depicted in *Monasticon Gallicanum*. *Reproduced courtesy of the Bibilothèque Nationale de France*

Although the traditional date for the foundation of the Premonstratensian order is given as 1120, it seems to have been in 1121 that Norbert himself began to consider the options for formalising the rule by which his followers were to live. He had many options from which to choose, with the hermit-like example of the Carthusian order, founded soon after 1100 by St Bruno, and whose style of religious life was acquiring formal structure at just this time, or the Cistercians, whose austere life of communal seclusion, labour and prayer was rapidly winning recruits across Europe, representing the two main traditions. The Cistercians followed the rule of St Benedict, a regimen devised for men who chose to live a communal religious life but withdrawn from the world as monks. The Carthusians, too, lived a life withdrawn from the snares of the world. While both orders' traditions had much to commend them, Norbert was drawn more to a life of preaching and missionary work in the world of men, an existence which neither orders' rules permitted. Instead, he favoured the rule of St Augustine, which had been devised as a system whereby priests could live in a communal, monk-like tradition as canons, but still operate beyond the walls of their monastery and serve as preachers, teachers and pastors. Nevertheless, Norbert chose to draw heavily on the Cistercian rule and incorporate aspects of its organisational system and austere ethos into his new order. His aim was to have his followers lead the apostolic life of poverty, simplicity and preaching, but in a structured, communal system. Before his plans had fully crystallised, however, in 1126 Norbert left Prémontré to take up the archbishopric of Magdeburg, the centre from which the conversion of the pagan Slavs east of the River Elbe was being directed and where his missionary fervour could be given free rein. His successors at Prémontré were more practically minded than he may have been and it was they who gave the Premonstratensians their more clearly monastic character.[7]

The rule which Norbert's successors framed was based chiefly on that which St Augustine had devised for priests who wished to live a communal life. Followers of that rule are known as Augustinian canons-regular, that is, canons who follow a rule (Latin, *regula*), or Black Canons from the colour of the habits which they wore. To distinguish themselves from the Augustinians, Premonstratensian canons-regular wore white habits, and became known as the White Canons (2). Although these Augustinians and Premonstratensians are labelled 'canons', in their organisation and style of life they were little different from monks, the chief distinction being that all canons were priests and they could serve outside the walls of their monastery while not all monks were ordained and, in theory, they could not leave their communities. Premonstratensians were even closer to monks in their practices in that they adopted the very strongly centralised organisational system developed by the Cistercians. This meant that, as colonies of White Canons were established across Europe, the Abbot of Prémontré became Abbot General of a network of daughter-houses and that he had disciplinary powers of supervision to enforce conformity of practice within them all. Abbots

2 A Premonstratensian Canon. From Dugdale's *Monasticon*

of the daughter-houses were required to attend an annual general chapter of the order at Prémontré and, for enforcement of discipline and conformity more locally, they were organised also into groups known as *circaries*.

It was not just this hierarchical structure and centralised control of the order which the Premonstratensians adopted from the Cistercians, they embraced also the monks' methods of estate-management and organisation. Like the Cistercians, the Premonstratensians made use of lay-brothers, or *conversi*, men who lived like monks but who had not taken full monastic vows and who were considered to be more suited to a life of practical work than one of contemplation and devotion. These lay-brothers provided the labour force necessary to fulfil as much as possible the monastic ideal of self-sufficiency, freeing their fully-professed brethren to concentrate on the spiritual life. It was the muscle of the lay-brothers that worked the land around the monastery, and which provided the abbey's outlying farming properties – or *granges* – with their labour.[8]

In selecting the Premonstratensians, Hugh de Morville was turning to an order that was less than three decades old. It was, however, expanding rapidly – some 120 Premonstratensian monasteries were founded within the first generation of the order – and, like the Augustinians more generally, was favoured by bishops and rulers in areas where the reform and reconstruction of religious life was being undertaken. The first Premonstratensian house in England, at Newhouse or Newsham Abbey in Lincolnshire, had been founded in only 1143.[9] Five years later, Eustace Fitz John, a friend and associate of Hugh's, brought a colony of canons from Newsham to Alnwick in Northumberland.[10] At that date, Northumberland was under Scottish rule, with Earl Henry, the son and heir of King David I of Scotland, governing it from Bamburgh and Newcastle. The presence of this new community would have been well known to Hugh, and it was probably visited by him when travelling to Earl Henry's court, or when visiting Eustace Fitz John's castle at Alnwick (3). Eustace, indeed, may have provided Hugh with the introductions which planted the germ of the plan to found his own abbey in his lordship of Lauderdale.[11]

What he learned about this new order must have impressed him, for preparations for the foundation of a monastery were usually a long, drawn-out affair and may have begun soon after 1148. Hugh was probably engaged in negotiations with the abbots of Alnwick and Newsham for a number of years, for they needed to be convinced that both a suitable site could be provided for a colony to be sent to, and also that adequate financial arrangements could be set in place for its future sustenance. De Morville's plans for the establishment of a monastery on his land reached fruition in 1150 when the monastery at Dryburgh

3 Alnwick Abbey, the gatehouse. From *Archaeological Journal* vol. 44

was formally founded at Martinmas (10 November).[12] This date probably marked only the drawing up of the agreement between Hugh and the canons of Alnwick which made over the land for the site of the abbey, set in place other financial arrangements for its future support, and set out what provision would be made for the erection of at least temporary buildings to house the new colony. There evidently followed a little over two years of further negotiation and preliminary construction work, until on St Lucy's Day (13 December) 1152 the founding colony arrived at Dryburgh under the leadership of their first abbot, Roger.[13]

EARLY ENDOWMENTS

As mentioned earlier, the actual foundation charter issued by Hugh de Morville to the canons has not survived but a number of early confirmations of their possessions made by Kings David I, Malcolm IV and William, and a bull of Pope Lucius III issued to the canons in 1184, which lists and confirms to them the properties granted to the abbey down to that time, allows us to reconstruct a general picture of the founding endowment.[14] According to these, Hugh gave the place of Dryburgh itself with land, woods, pastures and waters appurtenant to it; the fishing which he owned at Berwick; the two parish churches in his lordship of Lauderdale which he controlled, at Mertoun, with a carucate of land which pertained to it, and Channelkirk with the land pertaining to it; a third church at Asby on his Westmorland estates, with its pertinents; and the teinds of the mills of Lauder and of Saltoun in East Lothian. In comparison with the generous provision made for Kelso or Melrose at the time of their foundation this collection of items appears pretty meagre, but given the non-royal status of Hugh de Morville and the limited resources at his disposal it does represent a very significant portion of his disposable wealth.

Suitable buildings, too, must have been in place by December 1152 for the abbot of Alnwick to permit the colony of canons to leave his abbey and take up residence at Dryburgh (see below pp.47–48). These, however, were probably only temporary structures, sufficient to house the brethren and enable them to perform the daily offices whilst building operations continued around them. That aid with construction work remained a priority for the canons is perhaps reflected in a charter issued in their favour by King David, which, as well as confirming various small gifts of property made to them by Hugh's wife, Beatrice de Beauchamp, also gave them free licence to take without hindrance as much timber from his woods as they needed for 'their works and buildings'.[15] The canons had not arrived at a pristine monastery, nestling in seclusion by the waters of the River Tweed, but had entered something that must have more closely resembled a building site.

Hugh probably maintained a close personal interest in the fortunes of his foundation. He continued to make small additional gifts for its support and probably encouraged his family and vassals to do likewise.[16] It was in the later 1150s and early 1160s in particular that Beatrice made her various grants of property to the canons. Some elements of her gifts, such as the patronage of the church of Bozeat in Northamptonshire (see pp.165-166), formed part of her own property which she had brought into her marriage with Hugh,[17] but other items, including properties in and around the burgh of Roxburgh, she purchased specifically to give to the canons.[18] For Hugh, though, his support for the abbey was an investment for his spiritual future, and he was to demonstrate at the end of his life that his commitment to it went beyond mere fashion. Like several great noblemen of the time, Hugh eventually renounced his position of power and wealth in the world and entered religion, a move guaranteed to secure him spiritual salvation. In about 1162, he handed over his lands and titles to his sons, Hugh the Younger and Richard, the former gaining most of the English properties of his father whilst the latter acquired the more extensive Scottish lands, and was received into the convent that he had founded. Given that he was married and his wife was certainly still alive, he cannot have been accepted into full membership of the community. There, however, in the habit of a canon, he died later the same year.[19]

DIVIDED EFFORTS

Hugh's death proved to be more of a blow to the canons of Dryburgh than might have been expected for, although Richard his son and successor continued to show favour towards them, the new Constable's religious patronage was soon diverted to the hospital of St Leonard which he founded in about 1170 some 2km down Lauderdale from his residence at Lauder,[20] and on a far grander scale to his own monastic foundation, Kilwinning Abbey in the lordship of Cunningham. Hugh might already have possessed this Clyde Coast lordship before 1162, but it was Richard who seems to have established his family's interests there on a firm footing and the foundation of an abbey there represented a powerful symbol of de Morville ambitions. The loss of Kilwinning's cartulary makes it impossible to date its foundation with certainty, but sometime between about 1169 and 1187 is the most favoured time range.[21] Although it, too, appears to have been poorly endowed from the time of its foundation,[22] the monumental scale of the church at Kilwinning indicates that considerable expense was lavished on its construction. Some of that expense was met by gifts from the de Morville interest in Lauderdale, gifts that the canons of Dryburgh may have felt more rightly to belong to them. Kilwinning's interests in the church of Lauder resulted in a protracted quarrel with Dryburgh over the teinds due to the two monasteries and was finally settled only in 1222 by judgement of papally-appointed judges-delegate who instituted a formal division of the revenues.[23] Richard de Morville may have been keen to make his mark through the foundation of a second monastery by his family, but his ambitions produced two impoverished houses who struggled financially throughout their existence.

Some stability through this long, formative period in the community's development was afforded by the presence of Roger, the first abbot. He had led the colony from Alnwick in 1152 and remained in charge of its affairs until his resignation, probably on account of age and ill-health, twenty-five years later.[24] He was succeeded as abbot by the prior, Gerard, an experienced member of the convent, but by 1184 he appears to have been incapacitated by ill health and a coadjutor (assistant) was appointed to manage the affairs of the abbey on his behalf.[25] The man chosen was one of the canons, Adam, a scholar of outstanding intellect and spiritual renown, who held the office until Gerard's death or resignation in 1188.[26] Adam was Dryburgh's one great contribution to the intellectual achievements of the Middle Ages and his writings on monasticism reveal much about the religious experience of his fellow canons there.[27] Indeed, such was Adam's desire to achieve a more intense spirituality and closer focus on his religious devotions that in 1188, following a visit to Prémontré and a preaching tour which took him into Burgundy, he left the Premonstratensian order to join the Carthusians and became a monk at Witham in Somerset.

Throughout this initial period, Dryburgh appears to have prospered and, although its revenue base remained small, it appears to have suffered no difficulties in attracting a steady intake of novices to swell the ranks of the canons. Indeed, by the end of the twelfth century the number of canons had risen to the point where the existing buildings were no longer adequate to house them and where Dryburgh itself could send out colonies. Although it has been suggested that Dryburgh's colonies were established in the 1260s,[28] given the prolonged financial instability which afflicted the abbey throughout the first half of the thirteenth century (see below), and the waning in popularity of the older, established monastic orders in favour of the new orders of friars, it seems more likely that they were founded in the 1190s when the Premonstratensians were still at the height of their popularity. There is, moreover, uncertainty as to whether one or two colonies were sent out, how successful they were, and where precisely they were located. What can be established is that shortly before 1200, John de Courcy, lord of Ulster, removed a convent of Cistercian monks from the church of St Mary beside his castle at Carrickfergus on the Antrim coast and replaced them with canons from Dryburgh. This community, by the fourteenth century, appears to have been relocated to Woodburn. A second colony appears to have been established by de Courcy around the same time at Drumcross or Dieulacresse, also in Antrim.[29] Neither colony was successful in the long term, but their comparative failure was a consequence of the recurrent political upheavals in Ulster through the early thirteenth century and again in the early 1300s, rather than of the crises which afflicted their mother-house in the 1200s.

What direct connection John de Courcy had with Dryburgh which led to his going there to obtain the colonists for his foundations is unknown. It has been argued that he had strong family connections with Cumbria, through which he may have maintained ties with the de Morvilles, branches of whom held the baronies of Westmorland and Burgh-by-Sands during the reign of Henry II.[30] It is, however, a fairly tenuous link and there is no other evidence to show that he had any family connection with, or had shown any previous interest in, Dryburgh.

PLANNING BEYOND ITS MEANS

The same confidence which saw Dryburgh send out its offshoots at the end of the twelfth century also saw the community take the decision to embark upon an ambitious construction programme to replace their original buildings with something altogether more splendid (see below pp.48-50). Developments of this kind were fairly common around this time in the first generation of monasteries founded in Scotland in the twelfth century, and reflect the success of these older communities both in attracting recruits to the point that extra space was required to accommodate their large number and also in securing the flow of gifts from which the expansion could be funded. That Dryburgh was following the example of its neighbour at Melrose is no surprise, and underscores the confidence of a community who enjoyed the patronage of one of the wealthiest and most powerful families in Britain at that time, but their ambitions appear to have quickly outstripped the resources available to them. Building in stone and on a grand scale, such as the convent planned for their church at Dryburgh, was cripplingly expensive, and even better-endowed monasteries, such as Melrose, struggled to secure the flow of revenue necessary for a sustained programme of works.

It may be purely coincidental, but from the 1210s onwards the canons became involved in a succession of protracted lawsuits over possession of land and control of the rights to collect teind income on its properties. Several of these actions were raised in part to make use of the presence in Scotland in 1221 of the papal legate, Master James, who had the authority to make definitive judgements in disputes and to confirm charters. In April 1221 he spent some days at Dryburgh, where he gave judgement on a number of matters and issued the canons with confirmations of their properties and rights.[31] Much of this activity may simply have been 'good housekeeping' on the part of the canons, but there is also a hint of desperation to secure all possible sources of income. As building work dragged on into the 1230s and 1240s, as the architectural evidence seems to indicate (see below pp.53-73), the abbey moved deeper into financial crisis.

In 1240, possibly as a result of criticism for the indebtedness which had grown under his abbacy, the then abbot, Walter, resigned his office and was succeeded by John, a canon of the house.[32] The debts continued to mount as building work staggered on into the 1240s. On 21 April 1242, the canons' diocesan, David de

Bernham, bishop of St Andrews, granted them permission to appoint one of their own number to the vicarages of churches where the rectories were already appropriated to the abbey, citing various reasons but particularly '…since they have been burdened by grinding debts both on account of construction of the monastery and also on account of other and various necessities'.[33] Eventually, John too was forced to resign on account of his financial incompetence and on 13 January 1255, Pope Alexander IV wrote to the bishop of St Andrews and the abbot of Jedburgh, instructing them to apply all of the abbey's revenues to pay off debts which John had accumulated. The gravity of the crisis was underscored by the pope's order that they were to reserve only enough of Dryburgh's income to provide basic maintenance for John's successor and a minimum number of the canons, with the remainder of the convent to be dispersed to other Premonstratensian houses until such time as the abbey's debts had been cleared.[34]

Concern over the precarious position of the abbey's finances had clearly been growing for a number of years, and the Church authorities appear to have attempted a series of measures to ease the community through this time of crisis. In 1246, for example, Pope Innocent IV granted an indulgence of 40 days to all those who visited the church of Dryburgh on the anniversary of its consecration, an award designed to attract pilgrims to the abbey who could be expected to make offerings.[35] He also gave them a protection from obligations to make pensions or appointments to benefices that would represent a drain on their income, and a general protection for the monastery, the canons and all their goods against the depredations of all men.[36] The latter was perhaps of particular value as the level of debts mounted, as it shielded individuals responsible for running the affairs of the abbey, the community in general, and their property, from litigation or seizure. In modern terms, the abbey appears to have spent a considerable period in financial administration and enjoyed some of the benefits afforded by bankruptcy.

It would be wrong to think that the canons blundered blindly into the crisis and did little to help themselves out of the financial black hole which their ambitious building scheme represented. Indeed, there are some interesting indications of how the canons had attempted to boost the revenues available to them to pay for the building work in the first half of the thirteenth century. Existing patrons and local landholders appear to have been encouraged to make endowments, no matter how small, and were offered incentives to do so. In the late 1220s, Patrick, heir to the earldom of Dunbar, for example, granted for 'the new work of the church … of Dryburgh', one merk of silver from his rental income from Kirkinsyd 'to the building and repair of the church.' In return, Patrick and his wife were to be received into the fraternity of the canons and their souls would benefit in perpetuity from the common masses and prayers of the convent.[37] Soon after her husband's death in 1248, Patrick's widow, Countess Euphemia, confirmed the grant but stipulated that after her death the money should be redirected from the church fabric fund to pay instead for a 'pittance' to be served to the canons at mealtimes in the refectory on the anniversary of her death.[38] On an altogether humbler scale, between about 1210 and 1234, Everard the baker of Lauder gave 'one acre of arable in the ploughed field which is called Alriches croftys on the outer edge of that ploughed field and nearer to the land of my lord Alan of Galloway towards the north and one acre of meadow which lies within the outlying arable land towards the south' to help to pay for the 'new work of St Mary of Dryburgh'.[39] In about 1250, Isobel de Merlintoun, widow of William de Boseville, granted the canons an acre of her land at 'Brokislawe' in Newton, 'for the work of the church of Dryburgh'.[40] Cumulatively, small gifts such as these provided a much-needed boost to the over-stretched income of the abbey, and by the 1260s the worst of the crisis appears to have passed.

The remainder of the thirteenth century appears to have passed quietly for Dryburgh, its recovery perhaps aided by the buoyant economy of the period. While the abbey did not possess the vast expanses of upland grazing which provided the bedrock of the economic success of its richer and larger neighbours (see below pp.151–152), it lay in the heart of a prosperous region and drew much of its income from sources that were founded on the economic well-being of the wider population. As the economy of southern Scotland expanded through the 1270s and 1280s, Dryburgh benefited indirectly, but it was always a precarious prosperity.

PATRONS AND PROTECTORS

Amongst the many factors which had adversely affected Dryburgh's well-being through the first century of its existence, one had been literally fundamental: its origin as an aristocratic rather than a royal foundation. The importance of this distinction should not be underestimated, for it had ramifications that extended far beyond the obvious level of scale of the original endowment. Wealthy and powerful though the de Morvilles were in the twelfth century, the resources at their disposal were limited and, as we have already seen, they were stretched to breaking point as Hugh's heirs sought to spread their patronage wider. Only the kings of Scots and the independent rulers of Galloway had access to resources on a scale adequate to support such grand ambitions, and even then their generosity could be unevenly spread.[41] Dryburgh, as the product of a noble family of limited means, embedded in a region surrounded by better-connected monastic communities, was destined to struggle from the outset.

Further complications were added by the fortunes of the de Morvilles. In 1196, Hugh's grandson, William, died childless and the de Morville inheritance passed to his sister, Helen, and her husband, Roland, lord of Galloway. The Galloways were a significantly wealthier and more powerful family, who were semi-autonomous princes in their own right and related by blood to the kings of England. Dryburgh might have expected these new patrons to provide them with new endowments from which expansion could be funded, but Roland of Galloway was patron already of four monasteries founded by his family in south-west Scotland, including his own recent Cistercian foundation at Glenluce, and was also a benefactor of a number of other communities with which his family had connections, ranging from Holyrood at Edinburgh, to Holmcultram and St Bees in Cumbria.[42] Roland would support Dryburgh, but there would be no flood of fresh patronage.

Dryburgh's position as just one amongst several institutions competing for the benevolence of the Galloways received a further knock in 1234 when Alan, last of the direct male line of lords of Galloway, died. He left three daughters to succeed him and, after some upheaval, his great inheritance was partitioned between these heiresses and their husbands. Along with the rest of the inheritance, the de Morville portion was split and by the 1250s it was held by the two main beneficiaries, Helen of Galloway and her husband, Roger de Quincy, earl of Winchester, and Dervorgilla of Galloway and her husband, John Balliol of Barnard Castle. Again, these families already had established interests elsewhere and, with even the Lauderdale inheritance being divided between them, the pool of available patronage dwindled still further. Earl Roger and his wife, however, did make several grants to Dryburgh, including Gledswood on the Tweed north of Bemersyde, a fishery in the Loch of Mertoun, and a burgage in Haddington.[43] When the de Quincy inheritance was divided between a further set of heiresses in 1264, while the abbey was provided with access to an even more extended group of potential patrons, these were families who lacked any intimate association with Dryburgh and who had other priorities at which to target their religious patronage. By the 1260s, then, Dryburgh's only significant potential patrons were Dervorgilla and her husband, but the abbey appears to have found itself bound up in an inherited dispute with them over the patronage and teinds of the church of Lauder (see below pp.162-163). The bulk of Dervorgilla's religious patronage was also being directed elsewhere, with her own monastic foundation at Sweetheart in Galloway, and a number of convents of friars, receiving the main endowments.[44] She did, however, visit Dryburgh, it being there in March 1281 that she met with an English official to formalise her settlement of her English lands on her son, John Balliol.[45] While she may not have showered the canons with her benevolence, such visits imply that she was not altogether indifferent towards the abbey.

For the canons, levels of expectation may have been raised by the series of un-looked-for events which saw Dervorgilla's son propelled to the forefront of Scottish political society in the early 1290s, culminating in his elevation in 1292 to the throne of Scotland. After nearly a century and a half, Dryburgh had a royal patron. Ironically, if there were any prospect of the abbey capitalising on its royal connections it was snatched away from them within four years as a consequence of the collapse in Anglo-Scottish relations in 1295-6, Edward I of England's defeat and deposition of King John in the summer of 1296, and the forfeiture of the Balliol lands and titles. Not only had the link with the abbey's founder been severed, but it was quickly to find that this traumatic break was matched by a change in its overall circumstances. The comparative security – and benefits – which Dryburgh had enjoyed through its proximity to a fairly stable frontier was soon to be replaced by uncertainty and disorder as the Border districts were re-shaped into a contested buffer region. For the next two and a half centuries, Dryburgh lay in an exposed war zone.

THE ABBEY AND THE WARS OF INDEPENDENCE

On 28 August 1296, at Berwick, Abbot William of Dryburgh, together with the abbots of Jedburgh, Kelso and Melrose, gave their fealty to Edward I and their seals were appended to the formal document recording the Scottish submission, later known as Ragman Roll.[46] Having sworn faith to Edward, an instruction was issued on 2 September to the sheriffs of Berwick, Edinburgh and Fife ordering the restoration to the abbey of all its lands.[47] We do not know if Abbot William stood by his submission after the revival of the Scottish resistance to Edward in the Spring of 1297, but, given the general support which the Scottish Church gave to the efforts to restore King John at this time, it is likely that Dryburgh quickly threw its lot in with the pro-Balliol rising. From that point until 1316, however, we have little hard evidence to reveal how the abbey fared during the ebb and flow of the Anglo-Scottish conflict.

No record survives of how the canons of Dryburgh greeted the news that Robert Bruce, earl of Carrick, had murdered John Comyn, lord of Badenoch, in the church of the Franciscans at Dumfries and swiftly followed this up with his inauguration as king of Scots early in 1307. While Robert secured the backing of the bishops of Glasgow and St Andrews, many of the other senior clerics in Scotland were supporters of the Balliol and Comyn families and regarded him as a bloody-handed usurper. In common with many of Robert Bruce's Scottish opponents, these men were driven into the allegiance of the English Crown as the only realistic means of defeating him. Dryburgh, with its close links with the Balliol family, may have had more reason than most for failing to rally to the Bruce cause, but the fact that the abbey also lay deep in the heart of English-controlled south-eastern Scotland would have made any declaration of support for Robert foolhardy in the extreme. Its exposure to pressure from the nearby English strongholds of Roxburgh and Jedburgh, indeed, was underscored in 1310 when Sir Henry Percy, one of the key figures in the English military administration in Scotland, based himself and his retinue in the abbey.[48] There are no indications of tacit or open support for the Bruce cause from the heads of the Border abbeys throughout the bitter civil war years between 1307 and 1313, probably reflecting the fact that much of the warfare was being conducted north of the Forth or in

Galloway at this time. With the capture of Perth in January 1313 and Dumfries in February, the Bruce offensive began to push into Lothian and the Borders. By the end of 1313, the English occupation of southern Scotland had been reduced to a handful of isolated strongholds. Nevertheless, so long as Roxburgh remained in English hands, Dryburgh and the other Border abbeys continued to openly recognise the lordship of Edward II. When Roxburgh castle fell to a night attack by the Scots in February 1314, the monasteries were forced to make the decision which they had dodged for the previous seven years. Although no formal record of submission survives, it is likely that the abbot of Dryburgh was quick to come into King Robert's peace.

In the aftermath of Robert's victory four months later at Bannockburn, the pressure to submit on those Scots who still held to their old allegiance to either the Balliols or to the English crown mounted inexorably. Robert had made it clear that he was willing to accept men into his peace, regardless of their former hostility towards him, provided they renounced any conflicting fealties and homages. Essentially, you could either submit to King Robert and keep your lands and position, or adhere to the English king and lose all position in Scotland. Many found it a difficult choice to make and there were those who were not prepared to compromise their principles and submit to a man whom they regarded as a bloody-handed usurper. The choice was not limited to laymen only, for there were several prominent clerics whose loyalty still lay with the Balliol and Comyn families and who remained implacably opposed to the Bruce regime, but there were also lesser clergymen who could not make the demanded submission, including various Englishmen who held Scottish benefices or were professed of a Scottish monastery. It appears that the abbot and the majority of the canons at Dryburgh were prepared to accept Robert as their lord and king, but two canons, brothers John Dyttinsale and Hugh Dalnewick (whose name suggests that he may have come from Dryburgh's Northumberland mother-house) were expelled from the community some time before 21 October 1316 for their refusal to renounce their allegiance to Edward II. King Edward subsequently granted them all the rents and fishings of the abbey in Berwick-on-Tweed, for their support,[49] but they enjoyed that income for a very short time, for at the beginning of April 1318 Berwick was at last recaptured by the Scots.

Although Dryburgh had submitted to Robert there is, unlike at Melrose, no evidence that the king took on the role of patron and defender of the abbey. The king, however, did visit the abbey, basing himself there briefly in July 1316 when directing a series of Scottish raids into Northumberland and the small salient still controlled by the English around Berwick.[50] Despite that, the one surviving document which he issued while based there was in favour of Melrose. It is unclear why Dryburgh did not benefit from the king's patronage and it cannot be explained easily in terms of disfavour towards the canons on account of the abbey's Balliol associations, for elsewhere in the kingdom he was at pains to cultivate religious communities that had previously enjoyed close ties with the old regime. Quite possibly, Dryburgh was regarded as politically insignificant – after all, its landed holding was the smallest of the major monastic communities of the region – and therefore not worthy of cultivation. But Robert was hungry for any religious support which he could obtain, being keen to present a united front on the part of the Scottish Church and to project his own image as protector and restorer of that national Church in his negotiations to secure recognition for his kingship from the Papacy. The omission of Dryburgh from the list of monasteries which received Robert's patronage, therefore, which could be presented externally as a formerly pro-Balliol community that had recognised the rightfulness of the Bruce cause, seems doubly odd.

Regardless of whether or not Dryburgh occupied any position of favour with King Robert, its submission to the Scottish king made it fair game for English raiders. In July 1322, seeking to maintain the pressure on Edward II, King Robert had again invaded northern England and penetrated as far south as Stanemore and northern Lancashire before withdrawing. Edward, who had only just succeeded in reasserting his personal authority in his kingdom after a brief but bitter civil war, could not afford to appear weak in the face of this challenge, and in August he led a large invasion force into Scotland. This army penetrated as far north as Edinburgh but, deprived of forage and supplies by Scottish scorched earth tactics, Edward was forced to retreat south down Dere Street and through Lauderdale after only a fortnight. The retreating army burned Holyrood Abbey as it left Edinburgh, and when it reached Tweeddale, Melrose and Dryburgh, beside which 'in the playn' they encamped,[51] were both plundered and burned.[52] Unlike Melrose, to which Robert gave generously to finance its rebuilding, Dryburgh received no royal subsidy and was left to meet the costs of repair from its own resources. Indeed, the only sign of any royal concern for the abbey's plight was a brieve sent to the chamberlain in November 1325 by the king, who was then based at Melrose, ordering that an annual payment to the canons of 20 shillings from the burgh ferme of Roxburgh towards the lighting of their church, which they had received since the time of King William, should be made.[53] Given Robert's otherwise free-handed generosity to the Church elsewhere in Scotland, symbolised by his award of £2,000 from the royal revenues from Roxburghshire towards the rebuilding costs at Melrose, this denial of aid to Dryburgh again appears unusual and the 20 shilling rent derisory, but it does represent a continuation of his apparent indifference towards the abbey in the period immediately after Bannockburn.[54]

The canons, following the example adopted during the protracted building-operations of the thirteenth century, resorted instead to rattling the collection-box around local landholders. This brought some quick success, for while the king himself showed no readiness to aid Dryburgh his son-in-law, Walter Stewart, who held the patronage of the nearby church of Maxton, made over to them his rights in the church, the kirklands, and a further four acres of his land in the parish.[55] In February 1326, Bishop John of Glasgow confirmed the canons' possession of the church *in proprios usus*, which permitted them to divert its substantial revenues to their own needs 'on account of the burning of the church of Dryburgh and of its various kinds of destructions'.[56] It was possibly at this time also that the king's brother-in-law, Andrew Moray, conceded to the canons a piece of property in his lordship of Smailholm which had been a source of contention over ownership between them.[57] This support for the abbey from 'second division' royalty perhaps offers us an insight into Dryburgh's perceived status and again underscores its relative insignificance in Robert's designs.

Litigation to secure unpaid rents in Roxburgh may have been forced by the canons' critical shortage of funds to make repairs,[58] but once again it seems to have been chiefly smaller patrons who came to the rescue of the abbey. Through the late 1320s and early 1330s, the descendants of men who had made gifts to Dryburgh in the twelfth and thirteenth centuries gave a series of fresh grants, all apparently designed to bring additional cash income to the canons. Patrick, earl of Dunbar, for example, gave a scattering of lands and rights spread from Lauderdale to Dunbar, Sir William Abernethy and one of his vassals gave a series of small parcels of land and rents in Saltoun, while Henry Anstruther of that Ilk added to the gifts made by his grandfather and great-grandfather in the toun of Anstruther.[59] Their generosity, however, can only just have been beginning to deliver positive benefits to the canons when the Anglo-Scottish wars, which had only been ended by treaty in 1328, burst into renewed conflict.

Hostilities had resumed in early August 1332 when Edward Balliol, son of the deposed King John, with tacit English backing, invaded Scotland with a small army, defeated the much larger Scottish host at Dupplin in Strathearn south of Perth, and had himself crowned as Edward, king of Scotland, at Scone. The stunned pro-Bruce Scots had managed to rally in the autumn and drive Edward Balliol out of the kingdom in the course of the winter, but in the spring the would-be king returned with his now open ally, Edward III of England, and a major English army. While the two king Edwards settled down to besiege Berwick, the Bruce party in Scotland gathered its army and marched against them, only to be defeated again in a bloody rout at Halidon Hill outside Berwick on 19 July. As in 1296, the collapse of Scottish resistance after the defeat at Halidon Hill seemed total, and Edward III and Edward Balliol were able to march northwards through Scotland with minimal opposition, plant their own supporters in positions of power around the land, and receive submissions from men whose loyalties to the Bruce cause had always been shallowly rooted. English assistance for the Balliol cause, however, did not come cheaply, for in February 1334 Edward Balliol secured parliamentary agreement for the cession to Edward III of a huge swathe of territory, comprising the sheriffdoms of Berwick, Roxburgh, Dumfries, Selkirk, Peebles and Edinburgh, with the constabularies of Linlithgow and Haddington, and the forests of Jedburgh and Ettrick. Dryburgh was once more located in the heart of the sphere of English lordship in Scotland.

For Dryburgh, this change of lordship brought positive but short-term benefits, for the English crown and its administration in southern Scotland were keen to consolidate its hold swiftly and woo the influential regional landholders. The significant figure as far as the abbey was concerned was Sir William de Felton, who in July 1336 was appointed by Edward III as the keeper of Roxburgh Castle and sheriff of Roxburgh. Sir William became an active patron of the abbeys within his territory, and in 1338 purchased a valuable burgage in King Street in Roxburgh, which he then granted to Dryburgh, adding significantly to the canons' already substantial rental income from the town.[60] But such gains were only effective for so long as the English administration was able to maintain its hold over the Border region, and even by the mid 1330s that hold was becoming increasingly fragile. In 1334, Edward spent the main campaigning season in the Borders, mainly at Roxburgh, where he spent large sums of money on up-grading the defences of the castle. Little else, however, was achieved, and away from the main centres of the English occupation his position continued to be eroded away. He returned in the summer of 1335 with a large army which advanced from Carlisle to Perth, then withdrew southwards in September to Edinburgh then south via Dere Street to Tweeddale. In October, Edward planned to hold a council at Dryburgh,[61] expecting to receive an offer of surrender terms from the Scots as the result of the concerted military pressure brought to bear on them throughout the summer, but no approach came.[62] Further campaigns in 1336 and the beginning of a policy of rebuilding and strengthening fortifications in the occupied districts proved to be the high-water mark of Edward's offensive, and over the winter of 1336-7 it became clear that the tide had turned in favour of the Bruce party in Scotland. The English king, it was clear, had lost interest in a war that brought him no quick victory, nor any glory nor profit. As Edward turned his attention towards France in the spring of 1337, the security of the English-held buffer in Lothian and the Borders looked increasingly fragile.

Steadily mounting military pressure from the Scots between the return of David II from his French exile in 1342 and the autumn of 1346, when the king was captured in the disastrous Scottish defeat by the English at Neville's Cross outside Durham, had seen most of Roxburghshire and the western districts of Berwickshire brought back firmly into Scottish hands. During this brief period, however, the abbey was clearly considered to be under Scottish lordship by the Bruce Scots, as shown by Sir John Maxwell's grant and David II's confirmation of the gift to the canons of the patronage of the church of Pencaitland in East Lothian.[63] Whatever the political inclinations of the abbot and canons of Dryburgh, it seemed that they had been restored to the lordship of the Bruce kings of Scotland. Neville's Cross immediately reversed that situation, for in the winter of 1346-7 an English force swept up Tweeddale and re-established a garrison at Roxburgh, which quickly reasserted English authority over Teviotdale and central Tweeddale. Political reality again dictated that the abbey accept that it was under English overlordship, a position which was to prevail for over two decades. The abbot, like his counterparts in the other great monasteries of the region, appears to have moved comfortably into the relationship and seems to have accepted his role as one of the landed magnates of the English-held district south of the Lammermuirs. In this, he may still have been drawn by residual loyalty to the lineal descendant of his abbey's founders, King Edward Balliol, but it is more likely that pragmatic recognition of English power rather than vague loyalty to a discredited and ineffective cipher influenced him. It was as one of the vassals of the English Crown that on 20 January 1356, Abbot Andrew, together with the abbots of Jedburgh, Kelso and Melrose, witnessed the final act of Edward Balliol's long struggle to regain his father's throne, attesting the document in which Balliol resigned his whole right to the crown of Scotland into the hands of Edward III.[64]

SURVIVAL ON THE EDGE

Frustratingly, Dryburgh's own records of this tortured period in Scottish history have been lost, but the better-preserved records of Melrose Abbey allow us to see how the Border abbeys coped with their position in the midst of a bitterly-contested frontier zone. As part of the terms of his release from captivity in 1357, David II was obliged to recognise the territorial *status quo* in south-east Scotland. In the case of Melrose, he acknowledged that the abbey was 'through force and compulsion of necessity in the peace and faith of the English', permitted the monks to retain possession of their Scottish estates even although the convent had accepted the lordship of the English crown, and confirmed royal protection of their lands and rights.[65] It is likely that Dryburgh received a similar declaration of Scottish protection for its possessions in both the English-held region and within David II's territory, for there is no indication that its properties and rights were encroached upon at this time. David, of course, needed to keep Melrose and the other Border abbeys mollified for he required the customs duty paid on their substantial exports of wool to help him to pay the huge ransom that Edward III had demanded for his release. This motive was confirmed in 1358 when he granted Melrose the custom on all of its wool that it exported through Scottish ports, a move designed to divert as much of their produce as possible away from English-held Berwick. Dryburgh was never a wool producer on the scale of Melrose, and there is no indication that it benefited directly from a similar concession, but it is possible that it gained indirectly by selling its produce through the agency of Melrose. Certainly, Melrose was to develop its role as the main handler for the wool exports of many of the Scottish monasteries later in the fourteenth century.

Although the 1357 treaty which secured the release of David II from his captivity in England had provided for the temporary end of hostilities and the freezing of the current spheres of English and Scottish authority in the Borders, the 1360s and 1370s saw a continued erosion of English influence as Scottish lords, such as the earl of Douglas, strove to reassert their influence in territory which they regarded as rightfully theirs, displacing their English rivals, the Percys. Something of a 'phony war' developed as both sides attempted to maximise their interests in a region which still held great economic potential, with sweeteners being offered to producers and traders to direct their efforts in one direction or another. On 14 May 1373, for example, in a move designed to bind the Border abbeys more firmly into the English economic system and weaken their inclination to trade through Scottish-held ports in Lothian, Edward III granted them all the right to export 80 sacks of their wool through Berwick with the incentive of a discounted custom rate of half a mark.[66] David II, for his part, introduced officials whose duty it was to ensure that no Scottish produce from the Borders was traded other than through Scottish burghs and courts.

Despite the steady erosion of the English zone of control in the central and eastern Borders, by the close of the 1370s they still held the key fortresses of Roxburgh, Jedburgh and Berwick and considered Berwickshire and eastern Roxburghshire to be under their jurisdiction. When negotiations were entered into in 1380 for a settled border-line to be drawn up, the English king, Richard II, demanded that the boundary should follow the northern limit of Berwickshire, then descend Lauderdale with the Leader as the frontier to the northern edge of the Melrose estate, where it would turn west to Wedale, then descend from there to the River Tweed. Had that demand been accepted by the Scots, then Dryburgh would have been placed firmly within English-held territory. Instead, the canons found themselves in a military no-man's land between the main centre of English power at Roxburgh and Scottish influence in Teviotdale. It was a position that had disastrous consequences for them within a few years.

Through the summer of 1384 and into 1385, the Scots and their French allies steadily increased pressure on the remaining English-held strongholds in Scotland and began to raid deep into northern England. Eventually, in August 1385 the 19-year-old English king, Richard II, struck back and led a major invasion force on a devastating raid through the Borders and Lothian as far as Edinburgh, which he burned. Once again, however, the Scots refused to give battle and stripped the countryside of supplies, forcing Richard to head south after a campaign of less than a fortnight. It had, however, been two weeks of widespread destruction, for as the English army advanced northwards up Dere Street from Tweeddale to Edinburgh, Richard ordered his men to sack and burn the Scottish monasteries that lay along their route: Dryburgh, Melrose and Newbattle.[67] The brutality of this action has been roundly condemned by generations of Scottish historians and presented as another example of the wanton vandalism inflicted on Scotland by her southern neighbour in the course of their long conflict. It needs to be remembered, however, that in 1385 Scotland was a prominent supporter of the cause of the Avignon-based Pope Clement VII (1376-94), the rival of the Rome-based Pope Urban VI, whom the English supported. The Scottish monasteries were nests of schismatics and, therefore, fair game to the supporters of Urban. Furthermore, it was reported that the Scots had been using the monasteries as bases for operations against the English in the occupied territories, and therefore their destruction was a merited response for this ungodly behaviour.[68]

RECOVERY AND SURVIVAL

As at Melrose, the damage inflicted on Dryburgh at this time appears to have been extensive and the canons were faced with a potentially huge bill simply for repairs that would allow the convent to continue to function as a religious community. Given the financial crisis which the ambitious building programme of the early thirteenth century had brought, and the lack of any significant new endowments since that date, it must have seemed that the costs of basic repair work, let alone any more extensive rebuilding operations, lay beyond what could be met from their slender resources. Dryburgh needed a powerful patron and quite clearly the abbot must have begun to lobby hard with the political movers and shakers who pulled the strings of power in the kingdom. He was highly successful in his efforts, for he seems to have won the backing of the key figures in Scottish government in the late 1380s, Robert, earl of Fife and Menteith, Archibald the Grim, third earl of Douglas, and Walter Traill, bishop of St Andrews, who probably used their influence to secure the canons a substantial rescue package. On 9 March 1391, King Robert III issued a charter to the canons that brought them their biggest single windfall of property since the twelfth century.[69] According to this document, the convent of Cistercian nuns of Southberwick (Berwick-upon-Tweed), which had been founded by David I, was all but destroyed, its buildings collapsed and the place 'destitute entirely of both divine service and religious observance', and the two remaining nuns had '[thrown] off continence by slipping the bridle to indulge in acts of insolence and dissolution'. Since it was effectively moribund, the pious wishes of its original founder and subsequent benefactors had been frustrated and their gifts, instead of being turned to religious ends, were frittered away on the dissolute living of the sisters, so the souls of these former patrons were placed in jeopardy unless the nunnery's resources could be returned to their intended purpose. Consequently, the king granted all of the lands, rents and rights of Southberwick to Dryburgh 'to the honour of God and the increase of Divine cult and towards the rebuilding of the aforesaid monastery consumed a short while ago by hostile fire'. It seems at face value to be a straightforward reallocation of the resources of an effectively defunct community to aid in the reconstruction of another which had a functioning future but which was struggling to fund the rebuilding necessary after its burning in 1385. Of course, nothing could be that simple, and it is probably no coincidence that Southberwick at that date lay within the sphere of English lordship on the Border and, although technically still within the

Scottish bishopric of St Andrews, was subject to the Roman pope. The nunnery probably was in a parlous condition, given its location adjacent to much-fought-over Berwick, but it seems that the Scots were simply stripping the assets of what they considered to be a nest of schismatics. Although the award of the nunnery's property to Dryburgh was almost immediately challenged, with the backing of both the Duke of Albany and the earl of Douglas it was unlikely that the canons' possession was ever seriously in doubt.[70]

Although the chief flow of Black Douglas patronage was directed towards Melrose Abbey, the burial-place of the first two Douglas earls and a monastery with huge influence as a landholder in the heart of Douglas territory, Dryburgh also continued to benefit from the family's support, both direct and indirect.[71] In about 1420, Archibald, fourth earl of Douglas, 'considering the many and divers inconveniences which had befallen the monastery of Dryburgh, its abbot and convent', granted the canons the patronage of the parish church of Smailholm, which belonged to him as successor to the Morays of Bothwell, lords of Smailholm, and supported a supplication to the pope for the award to be confirmed.[72] In 1429, his son Archibald, fifth earl of Douglas, repeated the grant of Smailholm (valued at £20) and also petitioned the pope to ratify its annexation to the abbey, and also the earlier annexation of the poors' hospitals of Smailholm and St Leonard at Lauder (together valued at £15), of which he was also the patron.[73] These petitions were supported by Henry Wardlaw, bishop of St Andrews, who claimed that 'the fruits, rents and profits of the monastery by reasons of wars and divers other calamities were so scanty that they were not able to live from them and support the burdens incumbent upon them'. The petition was successful and the church and hospitals were annexed to the abbey, remaining in its possession down to the Reformation.

The flow of gifts to the abbey in the early fifteenth century must have helped greatly to pay towards reconstruction work after the 1385 disaster, but the canons continued to seek means of improving Dryburgh's financial position. In September 1432, for example, still claiming inability to meet the cost of repairs to the damage inflicted in the 'recent' fire from their existing revenues, they appealed to the pope to permit them to divert the gifts left by pilgrims to the chapel of St Boisil in Lessudden parish (St Boswells), the vicarage of which parish was served by one of the canons, towards the fabric fund of the abbey.[74] Other, less direct means of boosting revenues were also used. In January 1431, the heads of all of the Premonstratensian houses in southern Scotland appealed to Pope Martin V for conservatoria, or bulls of protection, to safeguard them, their monasteries, churches, men and vassals.[75] The protections were intended not only to offer a defence against attack by external enemies but were designed also to shelter them from litigation or physical attack by other Scots. In effect, it was a bid to secure a freeze for ten years on any costly litigation in which they were involved. Ironically, the efforts expended on securing this additional revenue were to be wasted, and only two years after the expiry of the ten-year conservatorium, fresh disaster struck.

In 1443, the abbey suffered a third time from fire, on this occasion apparently started accidentally.[76] The damage was possibly quite extensive, for as late as August 1461 the community was seeking fresh papal protection because the abbey had again been ravaged by fire, an appeal which implies that once more they were having difficulties in raising the capital to pay for repairs.[77] By that date, the abbey had lost the two influential patron families who had emerged to support it in the late fourteenth and early fifteenth centuries, the Black Douglases and the Albany Stewarts, and the lower-level patronage of other prominent local magnates, like the Dunbar earls of March, who had been forfeited in 1435. Once again, the canons were obliged to look to the lesser nobility for aid, but they appear to have found that fewer men than in the past were willing to dig deep into their own pockets to pay for repairs. Nevertheless, despite this further blow to monastic morale, as in the past the community managed to pull itself together and attempted to make good the damage. The quality of the repairs, however, suggests that enthusiasm – and the means to make good the damage – were in limited supply.

DEMORALISATION AND DECAY, c.1460-1560

Down to the second half of the fifteenth century, monastic life at Dryburgh seems to have been maintained and the community, despite the political turmoil and local aristocratic rivalries which surrounded it, had avoided the divisiveness of disputed elections engineered to promote the interests of one territorially ambitious family over another. The protection of the earl of Douglas may have ensured that Dryburgh did not fall prey to such machinations, although we should always be aware that the fragmentary record available to us might mask a more complicated picture in earlier years, but the overthrow of the ninth earl in 1455 and the collapse of the Black Douglas power structure in the Borders opened the door to the circling opportunists. As a result, in common with most other Scottish monasteries, the later fifteenth- and sixteenth-century history of Dryburgh is to a degree characterised by a succession of contested elections and shameless bids for control of the lands and revenues of the abbey.

The last apparently uncontested abbacy was that of Walter Dewar (1461-76),[78] but during his time the first clear signs emerge of the problems which were to beset Dryburgh in the years ahead. It is from Dewar's abbacy that the first evidence survives for the alienation of portions of the abbey's lands at extended tack. In November 1465, he sett the abbey's lands of Butchercots in Smailholm parish to William Haliburton of Mertoun and his wife for the term of their lives, for an annual rent of 40s.[79] The Haliburtons were kinsmen of the successors to the de Vaux lords of Dirleton, and it is possible that they had developed their Berwickshire interests through a link to Dryburgh originating in the abbey's East Lothian estates (see below pp.153-154). It is possible that Dewar himself had East Lothian connections, or at least he used his position as abbot to further the interests of his own kinsmen through a grant to them out of Dryburgh's property there: in 1479, Abbot Walter's successor, John Crawford, was pursuing an action against one John Dewar, who was allegedly occupying the kirklands of Saltoun 'bot [without] tak or sett'.[80] But while Walter may, on the one hand, have been feathering the nests of his own kinsmen, on the other he was actively seeking to recover revenues and lands which others had managed to appropriate from the abbey. For example, in 1473, he pursued, unsuccessfully as it proved, a court action against Lord Hamilton, accusing him of 'wranguiss occupatioun' of Dryburgh's property of Inglisberry Grange in Lanarkshire and non-payment of rents from those lands.[81] Three years later, he was seeking judgement against two men for 'wranguiss occupatioun' and cultivation for their own profit of the abbey's lands of Knockfield, and non-payment of rents extending back some sixteen years.[82]

The 30 years which followed Dewar's death saw a succession of men attempting to secure possession of the abbacy, their struggles also revealing evidence of factions within the monastic community. The first struggle was between two rival candidates, John Crawford and Hugh Douglas. Crawford was a canon of Dryburgh and secured his own election on Dewar's death, had his election confirmed locally, then obtained a papal confirmation by December 1477, for which he was paying his 'common service' or fees for appointment in 1479. Douglas, however, emerged as a challenger in December 1477. He was also elected nominally as a canon of Dryburgh, but he does not appear to have been a professed Premonstratensian at the time and was given six months grace in which to assume the monastic habit. He had, however, succeeded in obtaining provision from the father-abbot of Prémontré, which won him provision at Rome when Crawford attempted to challenge his right in the papal court. Nevertheless, Douglas was expelled from the abbey, whereupon in June 1482 he started further litigation against Crawford at Rome. When Crawford died in the course of that summer, Douglas was provided in his place, but himself died before even the papal bulls of provision could be drawn up.[83] It was an unedifying episode and revealed the extent to which external agents were influencing the internal life of the monastery. The convenient deaths of the rival abbots, however, did not bring an end to the turmoil.

In September 1482, the secular priest Andrew Lidderdale was given a grant of the abbacy with a three-month period of grace within which he was required to become a Premonstratensian canon, but in October he resigned in favour of one Thomas Hay. Hay was unable to secure his provision and Lidderdale appears to have remained in possession of the abbacy. The challenge did not end there, however, for early in 1483 one group of canons elected their own candidate for the position in John Fenton, canon of Dryburgh. Their argument was that Lidderdale's provision had lapsed because he had not assumed the monastic habit within the three months permitted to him. Fenton, however, soon found himself imprisoned by the supporters of one of his fellow canons, David Dinac, who managed to take control of the abbey during the first half of 1483. Dinac, however, was rejected by the pope in July 1483 and Fenton secured a papal confirmation with reservation of a pension from the monastery's revenues for Andrew Lidderdale. Nevertheless, Lidderdale evidently continued to hold the abbacy until December 1508, when he was deprived of the charge but provided with a pension from the abbey's fruits. The canons thereupon attempted to end the protracted instability which had disrupted their existence and have another of their number elected, nominating David Finlayson to the king.[84] James IV, however, had other plans for Dryburgh.

The closing stages of the long dispute over the abbacy of Dryburgh coincided with the opening of another dispute. This was over the primacy of the order in Scotland and was related to the efforts of the Abbot-General of the Premonstratensians, working with King James IV, to reform monastic discipline and adherence to the rules of the order amongst the Scottish abbeys. In 1505, Abbot Quentin Vaus of Soulseat was the only Scottish Premonstratensian head to attend a reforming Chapter-General of the order, and as a result he was appointed as 'visitator' of the Scottish circary and empowered to inspect the other monasteries of the order and enforce the improvement of standards. Vaus, as head of the oldest house of Premonstratensians in Scotland, may have felt that he was justified in taking on that responsibility, but his monastery was small, impoverished and insignificant, and the heads of the other Premonstratensian houses, especially the wealthy and powerful priory at Whithorn, were outraged and claimed the office for themselves. The result was a dispute which was settled by compromise in 1506 when the prior of Whithorn was made vistator, but with authority to permit Vaus to deputise for him. Further dispute followed, in which the Archbishop of St Andrews proposed that the Abbot of Dryburgh should be regarded as the most senior of the order in Scotland, possibly because the abbey was located within his archdiocese. His effort, however, failed, presumably because of the unsettled condition of Dryburgh and the fact that King James was preparing to nominate to it as commendator a lay cleric who could not function as an inspector-general of the other Premonstratensian monasteries.[85]

Instead of the long period of confusion and instability being ended by the appointment of a regular canon who could impose discipline from within, in 1509 the king appointed Andrew Forman, bishop of Moray, as 'commendator' rather than abbot of Dryburgh.[86] Commendatorships were an increasingly common phenomenon in late medieval Scotland, and were a device used by the crown originally to give control of monasteries to leading secular clerics. Most of the late fifteenth- and early sixteenth-century commendators were priests, but they were not usually members of the order to which the monasteries they were appointed belonged. The argument in favour of commendatorships was that the men appointed were powerful and influential individuals who could give the monastery strong rule and security. In reality, however, it was principally a device to award control of a monastery as a source of revenue to reward loyal crown service and, ultimately, was used by King James V as a means of providing for his brood of bastard sons. Men like Forman were unlikely to visit their commend regularly, if at all, and their primary concern was to ensure that the monastery provided them with a stable income stream. Designed in theory to reinforce or revive monastic standards, the commendatory system degenerated into a kind of legalised asset-stripping.[87]

Forman was a noted pluralist who had accumulated a substantial portfolio of Church benefices on his rise to power. Although he was a secular priest, in 1492 he used his connections at Rome to secure the promise of provision to the abbacy or commendatorship of the Cistercian abbey of Culross in Fife, but resigned his rights in 1493 in return for a large pension drawn from the abbey's revenues.[88] In 1495, he was given the Augustinian priory of May/Pittenweem, and was permitted to retain it as a commend following his provision to the see of Moray in November 1501.[89] Thus, when Forman was given the commendatorship of Dryburgh, he was already nominal head of the Fife priory as well as being bishop of Moray. Indeed, it appears that he retained control of Pittenweem until his death in 1521. Dryburgh was added to his portfolio in 1509 and in 1511 he attempted to secure the commendatorship of hugely wealth Kelso, but was never able to make good his provision.[90] He retained possession of both Pittenweem and Dryburgh after his provision to the French bishopric of Bourges in 1513, and added a claim to Arbroath after his provision to the archbishopric of St Andrews in 1514.[91] It was not until two years after he gained the archbishopric that he resigned Dryburgh.[92] Given Forman's prominence in Scottish political life, his career as a crown servant and role as an international diplomat, it is clear that he cannot have contributed in any significant way to the spiritual life of any of the communities of which he was the nominal head.[93]

Forman's successor as commendator was another secular cleric, royal servant and pluralist, Master James Ogilvy.[94] Again, he was effectively an absentee who was concerned chiefly to draw an income from his charge rather than involve himself in its daily life. His tenure of the commendatorship was short, admission to the temporalities of the abbey only being granted on 13 August 1516, nearly two years after which Forman had resigned them.[95] In the summer of 1518, the Duke of Albany, regent for the child King James V, wrote from Paris to Pope Leo X, notifying him of Ogilvy's death. He argued that what the abbey needed was 'a well-tried and forcible head, who can deal with a monastery going to ruin and suffering from lax discipline, and can repel the hostile attacks upon a place which is situated on the borders'.[96] His suggested replacement for Ogilvy was David Hamilton, bishop of Argyll, the younger brother of the powerful James, earl of Arran. The bishop was already involved in a lengthy appeal at Rome over attempts to provide him as commendator of the Cistercian abbey of Glenluce in Galloway.[97] How likely it was that the bishop would provide the strong and inspiring leadership advocated by Albany is highly dubious, but the political connections and military strength of his kinsmen were far more important to the Duke in his struggle against the earl of Angus than the real needs of Dryburgh. In May 1519, Hamilton, who had formally renounced his interest in Glenluce, was provided to the abbey as its commendator. For Arran, who held the regency during Albany's absence in France, his brother's possession of Dryburgh was a vital prop in the local alliances he was building against Angus, and in the summer of 1520 both Hamiltons were party to an agreement providing for amity and mutual support between the Hamilton affinity and the powerful Kers of Cessford and their network, which was designed to counter Angus's stranglehold on Borders' politics. As part of the deal, the Kers promised to 'maintain and defend' David Hamilton in peaceful enjoyment of the abbey.[98] His 'peaceful enjoyment' lasted barely four years and in December 1523 Albany was again writing to Rome to advise of Hamilton's death and to propose a new candidate as commendator.

In his letter, the Duke claimed that the abbey had suffered loss of its revenues and fire-damage to its fabric because of English raids, and needed an abbot who would restore the life of the community and bring its buildings back into repair.[99] His nominee on this occasion was another well-connected cleric, James Stewart, a canon of Glasgow, who was evidently a kinsman of the earl of Lennox. In February 1523/4, Stewart, describing himself as 'postulate of Dryburgh', wrote to his agent from Glasgow, reporting that Albany had given the presentation to the abbacy to John Stewart, third earl of Lennox, one of the key political figures in the minority of the young James V.[100] Lennox, Stewart reported, had 'disposed of it to him', in other words, he had probably sold it to the ambitious canon. The implications of this deal are at once made clear, for Stewart went on to instruct his agent to borrow money from bankers in Paris to pay for the papal bull that would confirm his presentation. Such borrowing would have been made against the security of the future income from the abbey: Stewart would have to milk Dryburgh for funds to repay the debts accumulated in his efforts to secure the abbacy.

James Stewart's cash needs would have placed a heavy burden on a community already struggling to recover from the damage inflicted in earlier raids. The position was made worse, however, for clearly there had been another aspiring candidate with powerful local connections, as Albany also requested that a pension of £100 Scots be provided for one Andrew Hume, apparently the brother of David Hume of Wedderburn,[101] from the abbey's revenues. The Hume family's interest in Dryburgh had been growing through the later fifteenth century and they had been one of the principal regional beneficiaries of the fall of the Black Douglases in 1455. In 1486, Alexander Hume had been appointed to the bailiary of the abbey, an office which gave him extensive powers of legal jurisdiction in the secular administration of Dryburgh's estates.[102] His kinsmen and wider network of dependents were, at this time, extending their influence in western Berwickshire, especially in lower Lauderdale where they held the lordship of Cowdenknowes, and Andrew Hume's appearance as a potential abbot or commendator of Dryburgh should be seen in the context of the development of their regional powerbase. Hume's candidacy certainly appears to have been serious, with the king writing on 22 March 1535 to the Cardinal of Ravenna at Rome, requesting that he secure papal confirmation of a life pension granted from the abbey revenues to Hume. In May 1536, Hume was beneficiary of a life-rent grant to himself and his illegitimate son of the kirklands of Lauder, in place of his annual pension, and in 1546 he re-emerged as recipient of a further grant of the teinds of the parish of Lauder.[103] This award was a compensatory deal designed to silence his claims, for he stated that he had been 'postulated' as abbot by the 'religious men of that convent'. It would seem, therefore, that the canons had attempted to elect their own abbot and that litigation between Lennox's nominee and the convent's preferred candidate had resulted in Pope Paul III eventually imposing a settlement which required Hume's right to be acknowledged by a financial settlement. James Stewart was then confirmed as commendator, receiving possession of the temporalities of the abbey on 6 October 1526, and led the house from then until 1539.[104]

It appears, however, that Stewart had little commitment to either the monastery or his religious vows. In March 1535, James V wrote to Pope Paul III to advise him that he had recently given Stewart the right to resign his position in favour of someone of his own choice. This was a major concession on the king's part, given the potential value of the abbey to him as an item of patronage. He had since learned, however, that Stewart was intending to resign in favour of his bastard son. In a breath-taking display of hypocritical double-standards, given James's systematic plundering of the Church to provide support for his large brood of illegitimate sons, the king denounced this idea as 'scandalous for the church and the king'.[105] The idea appears to have been abandoned, and the commendator remained in post until his death.

On 7 November 1539, James V wrote to Pope Paul III to nominate Thomas Erskine to the vacant commendatorship.[106] The nomination, however, was not formally accepted until April 1541, largely as a result of the rival provision to the abbacy of Robert Wauchope, a secular clerk and administrator of the Irish archbishopric of Armagh.[107] Despite complaints from James V and the king's refusal to admit him to the temporalities, Wauchope maintained his claims to Dryburgh down to 1545, when he was consecrated as Archbishop of Armagh. Erskine, who was a member of a family riding high in the king's favour at that time, took control of the abbey at a critical point in Anglo-Scottish relations as James V slid towards conflict with his uncle, Henry VIII. War with England finally erupted in 1542 and, while Dryburgh itself escaped a repeat of the plundering and burning which it had suffered in the early 1520s, its properties nearer to Kelso were ravaged in the great raid which the Duke of Norfolk led through the Merse. The abbey's luck seemed to hold through into 1544, when it again escaped the devastation inflicted on its neighbours by an English force led by Sir Ralph

Eure and Sir Brian Laytoun in February, a raid which had seen the destruction of Melrose.[108] Any celebration for this fortuitous escape, however, quickly proved to be premature, for in September 1544 the earl of Hertford launched what was to be a programme of calculated attacks on property throughout the eastern Borders. Late in the afternoon of Friday 7 November, an English raiding party arrived at Dryburgh and spent the next 28 hours systematically plundering and burning the abbey and the neighbouring township. The report of the operation describes how they '…rode …to a town called Dryburgh, with an abbey in the same, which was pretty town and well buylded; and they burnte the same town and abbey, saving the churche, with a great substance of corne, and got very much spoilage and insicht geir, and brought away an hundred nolte, sixty nags, a hundreth sheip'.[109] Hertford and his lieutenants wrote to Henry VIII from Kelso ten months later, informing the king that they planned to raze the abbey there and then proceed upriver to burn Dryburgh, Melrose and all the corn and villages on the way. Two days later, a further dispatch advised Henry that Melrose abbey and town had been burned, along with Dryburgh and 13 or 14 towns and villages, adding rather gleefully that 'not so much harm done these hundred years'.[110] Further fire damage may have been inflicted on those parts of the abbey spared in 1544, especially the church, but how much of value there was left to plunder in the monastery is questionable. These raids were not fatal to the community, but they came at a time when monastic morale was already low and it is unlikely that any significant effort was made to restore full religious life in the abbey before the Reformation swept away the old religious hierarchy in Scotland.

Thomas Erskine played an active role in the Scottish retaliation for this invasion, in 1545 leading a force of his own men in a raid into England.[111] His prominence in such military operations invited reciprocal attacks on his properties, but had more serious repercussions in 1547 when he was captured by the English. In late March 1547 it was reported that a Scottish warship, the *Lyon*, had been wrecked near Dover with heavy loss of life, but with many of its crew and passengers carried ashore and made captive. Amongst them was Thomas Erskine.[112] In April, Marie de Guise, the widow of James V, wrote to Edward VI's government in England, complaining of the detention of a gentleman of her household named 'Monsieur de Drebourg' who had been going to Rome on his own business, and was also undertaking a commission on her behalf to France. His capture, at the time of the loss of the *Lyon*, had occurred during a time of truce, so his release was demanded.[113] Edward finally responded, following a second, more strongly worded letter from Marie, in June, asserting that Erskine and his fellows were legitimate prisoners, but advising that arrangements for their ransom and release were being put in place.[114] Erskine, however, was still in captivity in December 1547, when he wrote to the earl of Warwick to request that his release date be deferred until he had received confirmation that arrangements for his ransom of £500 sterling had been set in place.[115] Payment of such a substantial ransom would have placed a heavy burden on Dryburgh, which would have been expected to contribute substantially towards the release of its titular head, and it was perhaps to release capital that on 25 July 1548 he resigned his position in favour of his brother, John, but retaining a pension from the abbey.[116] As late as 1551, however, he was still being described as abbot.

John Erskine's career was primarily in the world of secular politics and he displayed little commitment to his religious duties as administrator of the abbey. In 1555, he succeeded his father as Lord Erskine and emerged as one of the major figures in the turbulent politics of the reign of Queen Mary, who awarded him the Earldom of Mar. Although his ambitions clearly lay in a different direction, John held the commendatorship down to 1556 alongside his secular positions, but he finally resigned the abbacy to his nephew, David Erskine, the bastard son of his late brother, Robert, who received bulls confirming his appointment in July 1556.[117] By 1556, the Erskines' control over the abbey was well established and the commendatorship was acquiring something of the flavour of an hereditary office.

David Erskine presided over the last days of Dryburgh as a functioning monastery. As commendator, he oversaw the rapid alienation of large portions of the abbey's lands through feuferme grants to influential local lairds and men whose political support his family needed (see below pp.173-174). Certainly, he had no sympathy with the old religious tradition of the community placed under his charge and he emerged as a leading supporter of the Reforming party in Scotland in the late 1550s and early 1560s. He seems rarely to have visited the abbey, except when he required the remaining canons' signatures on feuferme charters, and in the 1570s he seems to have been mainly resident in Stirling. The accounts of his chamberlain, dated 19 December 1567,[118] however, do show that he was resident at the abbey for extended periods when he did choose to visit, and that money was spent on repairing the roofs and pointing the stonework of his 'chalmer in Driburgh the galorie and trance', indicating that he did consider it to be one of his seats of lordship.[119] His political career, founded on the wealth and territorial power which his possession of the commendatorships of both Dryburgh and the Augustinian abbey of Inchmahome in Menteith brought him, flourished in the 1570s when he was appointed one of the assistants to his uncle, the earl of Mar, who had been made regent for the young James VI following the assassination of the Regent Moray. Although Mar died within the year, the commendator maintained his active political role and by 1579 was serving as a privy counsellor. By then, he was becoming closely associated with the ultra-Protestant group amongst the nobility, and in 1582 he and his cousin, the second earl of Mar, joined with its leader, William, first earl of Gowrie, in the kidnapping of James VI in the coup known as the Raid of Ruthven.[120] The 'Raiders' held James for just under a year, but when he escaped from their control they were forced to flee to England. For his part in the episode, David Erskine was forfeited and Dryburgh placed under the control of a new commendator, William Stewart of Caverston.[121]

Stewart, whose possession was confirmed by Great Seal charter in August 1584, held the commendatorship for a little over a year before David Erskine was re-admitted to the favour of James VI and restored to his forfeited lands and titles.[122] By this date, the monastic community seems to have been effectively extinct, a comparatively rapid demise for a convent which only two decades earlier had been at least 10 strong. Despite the various vicissitudes of the house in the Border warfare of the early sixteenth century, it appears that recruitment of novices had continued at a healthy level into the sixteenth century. In 1537, in addition to James Stewart, the commendator, 16 or 17 canons appear as witnesses to charters.[123] By 1546, however, the names of only 12 canons follow that of the commendator and in 1554 it had dropped to 11.[124] On the eve of the Reformation, 10 canons are named and by 1562 the number had dropped to only nine.[125] In the space of 25 years the size of the community had apparently effectively halved, but it is not certain that all of the positions were vacant, with some of the incumbents possibly being absent from the monastery. In the 1567 chamberlain's accounts, when the remaining canons received their allotted portions from the income of the monastery, only four portions were noted as being vacant, but no indication is given of how many portions were allocated (see below p.171).[126] With further recruitment forbidden by act of the Reformation parliament and subsequent Protestant legislation, the continued existence of the convent was limited to the lifetime of the remaining canons. Only three were still resident in 1574, and the same three men continued to witness David Erskine's charters until they last appear in 1581.[127] On 10 June 1600, David opened a tack to one of his relatives with the comment, 'all the convent … now being decessit'.[128]

From that point, the continued existence of the monastery and a commendatorship of Dryburgh was something of a fiction. The process of winding up its four-and-a-half centuries of existence, however, only got formally underway in 1604 when the abbey and its lands were incorporated into the secular lordship of Cardross for John, second earl of Mar, but with David retaining possession.[129] When David resigned his office on 31 May in favour of his kinsman, Henry Erskine, third son of the earl of Mar, he extinguished the last link to pre-Reformation Dryburgh.[130]

CODA – AFTER THE ABBEY

Henry Erskine possessed Dryburgh as part of his lordship of Cardross and, although the monastery had been effectively converted into a secular lordship, continued to have the title of commendator until his death in 1628. He was succeeded as Lord Cardross by his son, David, who used the old abbey buildings as one of his main residences down to his death in 1671. Under David, however, the integrity of the former monastic estate, which had been held together by his father and his predecessors despite the various feuferme alienations, finally broke down. A large part of the estate was sold outright to the Haliburtons, whose interests in the abbey lands dated back to the fifteenth century. David's son, maintaining the radical Protestant tradition of his ancestors, was a determined opponent of the Episcopalian organisation imposed on the Church in Scotland by Charles II and James VII, and is reported to have held conventicles — illegal religious services conducted by those who refused to conform with the Crown's policies — in his house at Dryburgh. Arrested, imprisoned and fined for his religious beliefs, he sold the remains of the Dryburgh estate to Sir Patrick Scott of Ancrum, ending nearly two centuries of Erskine possession. After passing through various hands, in 1786 it was repurchased by David Erskine, eleventh earl of Buchan, a descendant of Henry, Lord Cardross. Buchan, a leading antiquarian figure of the day and founder of the Society of Antiquaries of Scotland, began the consolidation of the ruins that we see today, stabilising the structure and laying out the grounds around it as part of a romantic landscape to be viewed by visitors to his adjacent mansion. While much of Buchan's work may not stand up to modern expectations, his efforts ensured the survival of the ruins we see today (see below pp.136–140).

2

The architecture of the abbey

INTRODUCTION

Of the six Scottish foundations for the Premonstratensian order of regular canons, there are varying amounts of structural remains at four.[1] In the north of the country, much of the handsome small fourteenth-century abbey church has survived at Fearn, in Ross, and it remains in use for parochial worship (*4*). In the south-west, the shell of parts of the nave together with the heavily restored crypt at the eastern end of the cathedral priory church of Whithorn still stand (*5*); there are also reconstructed fragments of the poorly endowed Kirkudbrightshire abbey of Tongland (*6*). But of all the buildings at the Scottish houses of the order, those at Dryburgh are the most extensive, and were probably always the most architecturally ambitious, although what remains is no more than a fragment of the original.[2]

Idyllically located amongst hills within a loop of the Tweed, and now surrounded by mature parkland, the ruins of Dryburgh are a visual delight. The abbey has been additionally fortunate in the aesthetic and geological qualities of the locally available Upper Old Red Sandstone that was chosen for much of the building, which is mainly of a pinkish grey colour, and is capable of being cut into complex mouldings. It is thought most likely that the source of the best of this stone was quarries at Ploughlands, south of the Tweed, and about four kilometres east-south-east of the abbey (*7*), which also supplied some of the stone for Melrose Abbey.[3] Happily, Dryburgh's architecture is as rewarding to study as its buildings and setting are visually charming. The late twelfth-century east conventual range is one of the most complete monastic structures we have, while the eastern parts of the adjoining church offer fascinating – if highly tantalising – clues to the likely building sequence of such a large-scale house of prayer. All of this amply repays the effort involved in trying to understand the buildings.

The scant documentation which has a direct bearing on the building history of Dryburgh Abbey has been discussed in the earlier part of this book. In the

4 Fearn Abbey from the south-east. *Fawcett*

5 Whithorn Cathedral Priory, the nave from the south. *Fawcett*

6 *Right* Tongland Abbey, a surviving doorway. *Fawcett*

7 *Below* The quarry at Ploughlands. *Fawcett*

absence of such evidence, the best way of assessing the likely building dates of the component parts is by comparison with other buildings that are more securely dated, and this will be attempted in the course of discussing the various parts of the abbey. It would be particularly good to know something of the successive master masons who designed and supervised the construction of this magnificent complex of buildings, though such records as there are have preserved none of their names. One possible reminder of the otherwise unknown masons who built the Border abbeys is a grave slab that has been re-set vertically in the north wall of the presbytery. With a head of yellow sandstone and a restored shaft of red stone, it is incised with a pair of compasses and a set-square, the tools which were regarded as the chief emblems of the mason's craft, together with a sword that suggests a certain level of social aspiration (8). On each side of the head of the sword are what appear to be the letters 'a' and 'p' in Gothic script, while the blade of the sword is flanked by trails of ivy. Taking account of all the details, this memorial is unlikely to date before the late fourteenth century, the period when it is thought that Gothic letter forms began to be used for masonry inscriptions in the lowland areas of Scotland.[4] It would be tempting to speculate that this commemorated one of the masons responsible for repairs and reconstruction after the English attack of 1385. However, the stone was in fact found near Newstead, which may suggest it is more likely to have originated at Melrose. It was set into the presbytery wall by Sir David Erskine.[5]

8 Dryburgh Abbey, the mason's gravestone in the presbytery. *Fawcett*

THE LAYOUT AND LITURGICAL ARRANGEMENTS OF THE CHURCH

The site of the abbey slopes gently down towards the south, in response to which the main group of buildings around the four sides of the cloister had to be constructed on a series of partly artificial terraces. The church, the largest and most important building of the complex, is in the preferred location, on the north side of the cloister, where it did not block the sunlight from the lower buildings ranged around the other three sides. As a result, it is also on the highest ground of the area occupied by the surviving buildings. At its far east end was an aisle-less presbytery of three short bays, with an aisled choir of two bays to its west (9). Transepts of two bays projected laterally on each side at the crossing

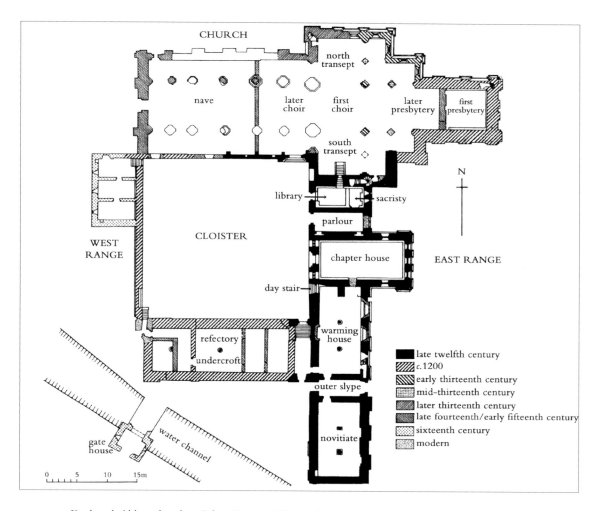

9 Dryburgh Abbey, the plan. *Sylvia Stevenson/Historic Scotland*

of the choir and the nave, with a chapel on the east side of the one bay of each transept which extends on either side beyond the choir and nave aisles; above the crossing there would have been a central tower. The nave was of six aisled bays in its final form, the two western bays being considerably shorter than those further east. The length of the nave may have varied throughout its history: there are indications that there were thoughts at one stage of reducing it to four bays; but it is also possible that the present six bays were not the original intention, and that the church was, or was at least intended to be, somewhat longer than we now see. In the layout of the eastern parts of the church it seems that Dryburgh followed the lead of its mother house of Alnwick Abbey in Northumberland,[6] where excavation in 1884 exposed what appears to have been a similar stepped plan of aisle-less presbytery and aisled choir and transepts (10).[7] It may be that the original intention at Dryburgh had been to have a nave of eight bays, as was eventually the case at the mother house; at Alnwick the thickening of the excavated footings at the west end of the nave may point to an intention to build a pair of towers over the west end of the aisles.

A number of doorways opened into the church, both from the monastic buildings and from the outside world. Within the south transept there were two small doorways at the lower level (11): one in the east chapel opened onto a spiral stairway which led both upwards to the higher levels of the church and the adjacent east conventual range, and downwards to the sacristy. The second doorway, at a lower level, led directly into the sacristy, and must always have been approached down a flight of steps; this opening has been greatly modified at a late stage. The largest of the doorways in the south transept was at an elevated level, part-way down the stairway which descended from the canons' dormitory on the first floor of the east conventual range. This stair and doorway was for

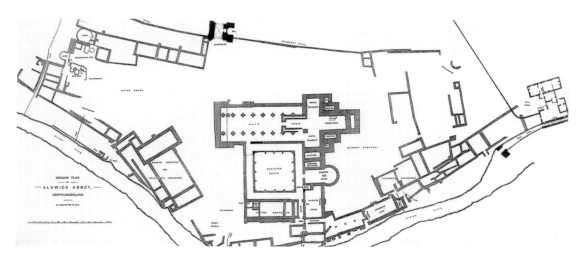

10 Alnwick Abbey, the plan. From *Archaeological Journal* vol. 44

11 Dryburgh Abbey, the south transept gable wall. © *Crown copyright, reproduced courtesy of Historic Scotland*

night-time access to the church. The canons would descend at about 2.30 a.m. in winter or 1.30 a.m. in summer for preliminary prayers and the office of Matins, probably returning to the dormitory again immediately afterwards in winter, or after the subsequent office of Prime in summer. They would again descend the night stair for Prime in winter or Lauds in winter. The final return to the dormitory was after Compline, which is thought to have been at about 6.30 p.m in winter or 8.15 p.m. in summer.[8]

For the canons' day-time use it was usual to have two doorways between church and cloister, in the south wall of the nave, the locations of which were largely in response to the requirements of the processions around church and cloister on Sundays and major feast days. One of those openings was usually aligned with the east cloister walk, and it was through that doorway the processions left the church to pass around the claustral ranges; the other was usually aligned with the west walk, and it was through that doorway the processions returned to the church to take up their stations in the nave before processing through the rood screen and pulpitum into the choir. Both doors could, of course, also be used for more mundane purposes. At Dryburgh, however, there have been three doorways in the south wall of the nave, though one of them may have been cut at a time when it was intended the nave should be truncated, perhaps being then walled up soon after being built. There were two further doorways into the church from the area outside the cloister: in the west front was the great processional entrance, which was probably only used by the most important visitors and on the most solemn occasions, and there was a smaller doorway, which could presumably be used by those layfolk who had access to the church, towards the west end of the north aisle wall.

Both the architectural forms and the usage of the church are likely to have been modified in various ways and on a number of occasions in the course of its life. Initially the high altar, the main focus of the canons' worship, was probably close to the east wall of the presbytery, and many other furnishings would have been provided within its vicinity to enhance the setting for the celebration of mass. These would have included sedilia, where the priest and his assistants were able to sit for certain parts of the service, a piscina, where the vessels used at mass could be cleansed, and lecterns for the books of gospels and epistles. Eventually there may also have been a sacrament house or a pyx where a consecrated host, believed to have become the body of Christ through the process of transubstantiation, could be reserved for veneration. There might also be an Easter Sepulchre, where Christ's death and burial could be re-enacted through the ritual entombment of his image together with a consecrated host between Good Friday and Easter Sunday. Some of these furnishings would be permanent fixtures of stone, timber or metal, though others might be more portable, and be brought in for the occasion, as required.[9]

At some stage the two eastern bays of the presbytery were cut off by a wall, which may have risen to no more than a few metres in height, with the space behind it being presumably put to use either as a new sacristy or as a chapel. There are certain parallels here with Alnwick, where it seems that a narrower eastern slice of the presbytery was also cut off by a cross wall. It may be assumed that, after the insertion of this wall at Dryburgh, the high altar would have been re-located within what had been the western bay of the aisle-less presbytery, with the richly decorated altarpiece behind it rising set against the new wall. During their daily round of services, the canons would have sat in two rows of timber stalls which faced each other across the main space of the choir, and turned at ninety degrees against a screen that would have separated off the choir from the rest of the church to the west. Initially those stalls are perhaps most likely to have been placed within the western bay of the aisled section of the choir, probably extending down from there into the crossing area below the tower. Low walls, of which footings survive in the western bay of the south choir arcade, may have been provided as the backing for the stalls.

If the choir stalls were located in that way, the screens that would have enclosed the west end of the choir are most likely to have been in the first bay of the nave. The eastern screen, the pulpitum, with its single central doorway, would probably have been within the west crossing arch. There may then have been a second screen, of either stone or timber, one bay further west. This second screen would have been the rood screen, having the church's main carving or painting of Christ's crucifixion above it; cut-back tusks of stone projecting from an internal buttress of the south nave wall, one bay west of the crossing, could be the enigmatically slight relics of this screen. The rood screen usually had two doorways opening towards the nave, with the main nave altar between them. The possibility that the screens were initially in this position may be supported by the provision of a trifoliate-arched piscina of early thirteenth-century type in the second bay from the east of the south nave wall. There it could have served a rood altar in that bay. However, when the east end of the presbytery was cut off by a wall, the choir must at the same time have been moved westwards, presumably extending down from the crossing into the two eastern bays of the nave. The partial footings of a stone screen wall with the threshold of a central doorway, which cross the nave two bays west of the crossing, presumably survive from the re-located pulpitum. To serve the altar or altars in front of this later screen, a second, and clearly later, piscina was inserted in the third bay from the east of the south nave aisle wall, the head of which has been truncated in the course of modern works of consolidation to the upper internal walls.

A major church also required considerable numbers of side altars, particularly when, as at Dryburgh, it was served by a community of canons in priestly orders, who were required to celebrate mass regularly, and ideally on a daily basis. These altars would have been dedicated to aspects of the godhead or to one or more saints. In addition to the high altar and the rood altar, the church was designed to have two architecturally distinct chapels with altars on the east side of each transept. The location of the altars in the chapels on the north side is confirmed by the way in which the wall shafts to the east walls of those parts start above a string course at mid-height of the wall, rather than at ground level, so that the altars could be set directly against the walls. In the north transept chapel there is also a trifoliate-headed piscina with a fluted basin, to the south of the altar site. But there were almost certainly several other altars either within the nave aisles or against the arcade piers, some of which may have been enclosed by timber screens. In the course of the Middle Ages there was a tendency for increasing numbers of altars to be founded, many of which are likely to have been endowed by benefactors who wished to have chantry masses celebrated at them, in an effort to ensure their salvation through the repeatedly offered prayers of the canons.

THE EARLIEST BUILDING FRAGMENTS

One of the many puzzling aspects of the buildings at Dryburgh is that, although the abbey was founded in 1150, there is nothing in the surviving buildings that could be firmly identified as dating from before the later decades of the century.

This presumably means that, for as much as three decades, the community must have occupied buildings earlier than those we now see. These could have been of timber construction, like those for which evidence has been found in the course of archaeological investigations below the later masonry structures of a number of English Cistercian abbeys, including Fountains and Sawley, for example.[10]

However, there is one clue which could point to the possibility that smaller scale structures of stone had been started, if not completed, in advance of the buildings we now see. This is to be seen at the junction of the east wall of the sacristy and parlour in the east conventual range, and of the south and east walls of the chapel on the east side of the adjacent transept. In this area there is masonry in the lower part of the walls which, while relatively carefully squared, is laid more unevenly and with wider joints than the rest of the walls (*12* and *13*). It is also particularly significant that there are no moulded base courses at the bottom of these walls, despite the fact that elsewhere there are base courses that are very carefully scaled and detailed in proportion to the walls they support. It is additionally striking that the fragmentary relic of a base course that does survive on the south side of the transept chapel is at a height of almost 2m above ground level, rather than at the base of the wall, as was usual. It may also be worth noting internally in this area that the north-facing respond at the junction of the transept chapel and choir aisle, which is in the form of a triplet of wall shafts, starts a short way above the present ground level, and is unsupported by any masonry directly below its base, as if it had been built above an existing fragment of wall (*14*). The gap below its base would probably have been hidden when the floor was paved, but is left visible now that the floor is gone.

Inevitably, at a building that is so extensively ruined, insufficient survives to be able to offer a firm interpretation of the evidence for changes in the character of the masonry at this junction of church and conventual buildings. All that can be said is that there is walling in this area, at a low level in relation to both the church and the adjacent east conventual range, that appears to be earlier than anything else now to be seen. It is one possibility – and perhaps a good possibility – that it survives from a church and conventual buildings started for the canons around the time of their first introduction to the site in 1152, with the intention that these should be replaced by the more ambitious buildings we now see when the opportunity arose.

THE BUILDING OF THE EXISTING CHURCH

As an unbroken round of worship was the main justification for the existence of any community of monks or canons, a place where that worship could be offered with sufficient dignity was the most essential structure at all monasteries. A building that could be consecrated for use as a church therefore had to be provided from the start, and that first church might sometimes remain in use

12 Dryburgh Abbey, the early masonry at the junction of the east conventual range and the south transept chapel. *Fawcett*

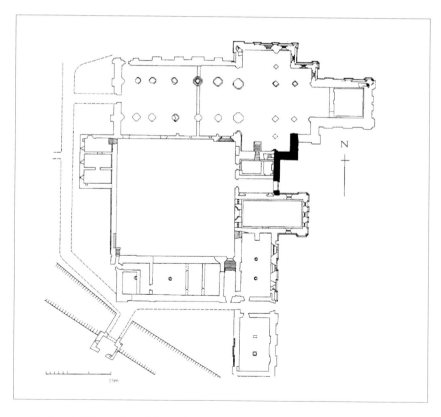

13 Dryburgh Abbey, plan of the early masonry at the junction of the east conventual range and the south transeptal chapel. *Sylvia Stevenson/Historic Scotland*

14 Dryburgh Abbey, the north-facing respond at the junction of the south choir and transept chapels. *Fawcett*

even while new and larger buildings were going up around it. At Dryburgh, it is particularly likely that the first church must have been on an adequate scale to meet the continuing needs of the canons, because there is little doubt that, once construction of the buildings we now see was started in earnest, it was the erection of the canons' domestic quarters in the east conventual range that was pressed ahead most rapidly, with building of the church held back. This could only have been contemplated if there was a church that was still at least adequate for the community's short-term needs.

Ideally, it might be better for the readers of this book if we could discuss the construction of the abbey's buildings in a strictly chronological manner. However, this would mean moving backwards and forwards through the buildings in a way that would be potentially confusing. In the hope of achieving some clarity of description, the existing church and monastic buildings will therefore be discussed separately, and, since the church was the most important building of the abbey, it will be dealt with first, despite the fact that it was evidently not the part on which the greatest energy was first expended once building works gathered momentum.

THE FIRST BUILDING PHASE OF THE CHURCH

Although it has just been suggested that construction of the east conventual range was pressed ahead more rapidly than work on the church, the architectural evidence leaves little room for doubt that, at the start of the great campaign of erecting the buildings we now see, the east range and eastern parts of the church had been laid out as part of the same operation. This is seen in the fact that the same base course, the mouldings at the foot of walls that gave major medieval buildings the appearance of being well founded, and that were inevitably the first part of any wall to be built, was used in both parts (*15A*). On the east side of the east range the base course only starts on the north side of the projecting section of the chapter house, and thus to the south of what it has been suggested was retained earlier masonry in the lower walls of the sacristy and parlour; it then continues all the way along the east face of the surviving section of the range, and is repeated on the west side of the part of the range that projects beyond the cloister. This base course consists of a sequence from bottom to top of a narrow chamfer and then a broader chamfer, below a keeled (pointed) roll and a very narrow top chamfer.

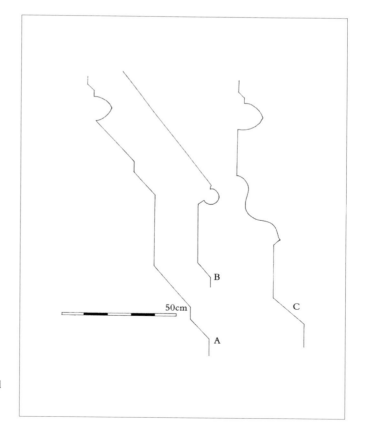

15 Dryburgh Abbey, measured sections of base courses: A. below the eastern parts of the choir and north transept (and below the east conventual range in reduced form); B. below the west side of the north transept and the east bay of the north nave aisle; C. below the west front and the west bay of the north nave aisle. *Fawcett*

There are the fragmentary stubs of what can be seen to have been the same type of base course set at an unexpectedly high level of the south wall of the south transept chapel, at its junction with the sacristy (see *12*). As already said, the high position of this base course is a factor that might be seen as offering additional support for the conclusion that earlier masonry was being retained at the lower levels in this area. Unfortunately, along the east side of the south transept chapel, the south and east sides of the south choir aisle and the south and east sides of the presbytery, the facing masonry of the wall, including the base course, has been almost entirely robbed away, but on the north side of the presbytery it becomes clear that we once again have the same base course as along the east range (*15A* and *16*).[11] Here the base course is scaled to the greater height of the church, and is elevated above an additional pair of chamfers that were already foreshadowed in the stubs on the south side of the south transept chapel. Having once re-appeared at the north-east corner of the presbytery the base course then runs continuously around the north side of the presbytery, the north choir aisle and transept chapel, and the north face of the north transept, stopping against the stair turret at the north-west corner of the transept, where a new type of base course was introduced (*17*).

On this evidence, there can be little doubt that the east conventual range and the eastern parts of the church were indeed laid out as part of the same building operation, probably in the last years of the twelfth century. In doing so, however,

16 Dryburgh Abbey, the base course at the north-east angle of the presbytery. *Fawcett*

17 Dryburgh Abbey, the junction of the two types of base course at the north–west angle of the north transept. *Fawcett*

extents of masonry from what it has been suggested were earlier buildings were retained in the lower walls at their junction, in a way that could be consistent with parts of those earlier buildings having been retained in use for a while. Once the foundations and lowest courses of the eastern parts of the church had been set out, however, we shall find evidence that the progress of building the church was far from smooth, and it seems that the endowments of the abbey, combined perhaps with some financial incompetence on the part of the abbot, were simply not equal to such high architectural ambitions (see above pp.16–18).

Nevertheless, since work on the east range was being pushed ahead in advance of the main body of the church, it was unavoidable that at least those parts of the church immediately adjoining the range had to be built up along with the range, and there are clear indications that they were indeed earlier than the rest of the church. Thus, we can see that the badly damaged and partly rebuilt doorway to the stair off the south transept chapel has saw–tooth–like chevron (zig-zag) decoration round its arch (*18*), of a pattern like that to be found around two of the windows towards the southern end of the east face of the adjacent conventual range (*90*). The external capitals of the window above it are also of a relatively early type, each having water-leaf foliage below a square abacus (*19*). Further pointers to a relatively early date for the parts of the church adjacent to the east range are seen in the form of the responds (half-piers) built in with the walls of the south transept chapel

18 Dryburgh Abbey, the south respond of the south transept arcade. *Fawcett*

19 Dryburgh Abbey, the window of the south transept chapel. *Fawcett*

and choir aisle; these are in the form of triplets of shafts, the leading element of which is keeled (20A), which rise from widely spreading water-holding bases (35B). In the south transept chapel the shafts are attached to a broad pilaster. The respond towards the choir aisle is particularly intriguing, since, as already mentioned, it starts slightly above the present ground level, supporting the idea that it may have been constructed over an existing wall fragment (see 14).

The great round-arched doorway in the first bay of the south nave aisle wall, which faced along the east walk of the cloister, and was the main processional exit from the church to the cloister, was probably also built as part of the same extended operation as the east conventual range and the lower parts of the south transept (21 and *colour plate 4*). Regrettably, our ability to understand it has been clouded as a consequence of a number of changes that it has undergone. These included the removal of its two inner orders at a date before 1788 (see *106*), so that they could be adapted as a landscape feature at the house of Newton Don; it was only in 1894 that they were returned to Dryburgh, and it is by no means certain that there have not been significant modifications in the process of dismantling and subsequent reconstruction. As it now stands the opening of the doorway is framed by an engaged inner order with paired bands of massive dogtooth decoration at right angles to each other, running around both

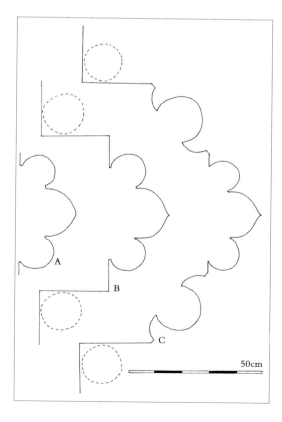

20 Dryburgh Abbey, measured sections of responds: A. in the south choir and transept chapels; B. at the east ends of the choir arcades; C. at the north end of the north transept arcade. *Fawcett*

21 Dryburgh Abbey, the doorway from the east cloister walk to the nave. © *Crown copyright, reproduced courtesy of Historic Scotland*

jambs and arch, and around this are three orders of arch mouldings carried on free-standing shafts set against angled masonry. All the orders rise from widely spreading water-holding bases. On the east side of the doorway the capitals of all of these orders have simple small foliate crockets below square abaci (22), which represent a slightly more complex variant on the water-leaf capitals of the closely related chapter house doorway (see below p.78). On the west side, however, the capitals have tightly organised blocks of foliage decoration of types that are essentially like stiff-leaf in having triplets of lobe-like leaves to each stem, or that are like multi-leafed ferns (23). These perhaps show partial parallels with the capitals of the southern doorway of the great trio of west front portals at Kirkwall Cathedral, where the foliage is similarly densely packed (24).

THE PRESBYTERY

Since so little survives of the church we must be very cautious in attempting to extrapolate the overall forms of the first design, though there is enough to suggest that a number of changes of detailing were introduced in the course of what was clearly a rather protracted and periodically interrupted building operation.

22 Above
Dryburgh Abbey,
the capitals on the
east side of the
doorway from the
east cloister walk
into the nave.
© Crown copyright,
reproduced courtesy
of Historic Scotland

23 Right
Dryburgh Abbey,
the capitals on the
west side of the
doorway from the
east cloister walk
into the nave.
© Crown copyright,
reproduced courtesy
of Historic Scotland

24 Kirkwall Cathedral, the west doorway capitals. *Fawcett*

As the location for the high altar, and thus the liturgically most important part, the aisle-less presbytery was presumably the first portion to be taken up to full height, once the parts adjacent to the east range had been completed. Externally its flanks were divided by pilaster buttresses into three narrow bays, while the excavated footings of the robbed external east face suggest that the east front was articulated by buttresses into three even narrower sections; there was a spiral stair to the upper storeys in the north-east corner. Internally, a continuous band of decorative arcading ran around the lowest level, which rose from a projecting stone bench. The best evidence for this arcading is now to be seen at the south-east corner, where there is a shaft and the ghosting of an arch (*25*); but most of the arcading was removed in the later Middle Ages, almost certainly as part of the repairs necessitated by one of the English attacks.

The stump of the north presbytery wall where it adjoined the choir chapel shows that there were two storeys of windows along the presbytery flanks, a horizontal division that presumably also continued along the east wall (*26*). Resting on a string course above the decorative arcading was the lower tier of windows, consisting of tall single-light openings, one to each bay, which rose through the arcade and gallery storeys of the adjacent aisled choir. The arches of these windows were of two orders both internally and externally. The outer order was supported by disengaged shafts in two stages, with shaft rings between the two stages, while the inner order was splayed, narrowly to the exterior, but far more broadly to the interior. The glazing would have been set in frames located within a rebate on the inner side of the windows. Above this level were the clearstorey windows, on the outer face of a wall passage which presumably

25 Dryburgh Abbey, the traces of blind arcading at the south east corner of the presbytery. *Fawcett*

26 Dryburgh Abbey, the north side of the choir and presbytery. © *Crown copyright, reproduced courtesy of Historic Scotland*

ran continuously around the whole church. There would have been a single small window on the outer face of each bay, aligned vertically with the taller windows at the lower level, and on the inner side of the passage was open arcading. In each of the narrow presbytery bays there were probably three arches to the arcading at this upper level, the central one corresponding to the window, the outer two in front of the flanking walls. In the three very narrow subdivisions of the east presbytery wall, which would have provided the original backdrop to the high altar, the windows must have been very tightly spaced, and it is likely that there would have been only one arch to the arcade on the inner side of the upper tier of windows, rather than the three of the side walls.

We now have no way of knowing how the high space of the presbytery was covered. It is certain that there was no stone vaulting, since this would have left traces of itself in the surviving fragment of clearstorey. Perhaps the most likely covering would have been an arched or polygonal timber barrel ceiling, formed within the timbers of the roof structure that rose from the wall-head. Ceilings of this kind are known to have existed at a number of major thirteenth-century churches.[12] The ghost of one is still to be seen against the east gable of Elgin Cathedral, for example, where it was presumably installed as part of the extensions following the fire of 1270 (27);[13] and a heavily restored example, with a slightly

27 Elgin Cathedral, the east wall. The ghosting of a barrel ceiling can be seen around the circular window. *Fawcett*

cusped profile and a plethora of surface ribbing, is still to be seen over the choir of Glasgow Cathedral, where it is part of the work started in the mid-thirteenth century (28).[14] If Dryburgh had a ceiling of similar form, it would have created an arched section at the top of the internal east wall of the presbytery, within the gable, which would certainly have been pierced by some form of opening. One possibility is that the clearstorey windows would themselves have risen up in an echelon grouping into that arched section, as at Glasgow, though it is equally possible that there would have been a third tier of windows, either in the form of a triplet of single-lights, reflecting those at the lower level, or in the form of a circular window, as at Elgin.

The architectural details of this aisle-less easternmost part of the church would probably fit best in the very early years of the thirteenth century. Some idea of how it may have looked when complete can be gained by comparison with the north and west sides of the roughly contemporary north transept at Hexham Priory in Northumberland, which similarly has an internal sequence from floor to roof of decorative blind arcading, a tier of tall windows, and a tier of rather more squat windows at clearstorey level (29). The main differences between the two buildings are that Hexham has mural passages to both levels of windows, and is now covered by a later open-timber roof of relatively flat section. Comparisons

28 Glasgow Cathedral, the choir. *Fawcett*

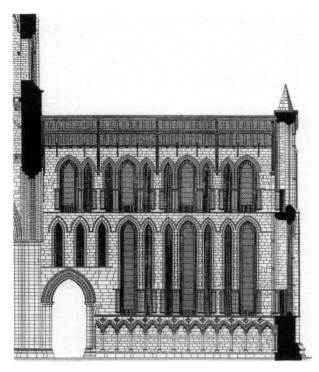

29 Hexham Priory, the west wall of the north transept. Hodges, *Hexham Priory*

30 Tynemouth Priory, the south flank of the presbytery. *Fawcett*

might also be made with the presbytery of Tynemouth Priory, though there the detailing is rather more enriched, and the clearstorey is designed to take high stone vaulting, with wall ribs embracing the window openings (*30*).

THE CHOIR AND TRANSEPTS

The north side of the choir and the east side of the north transept are the most intact parts of the abbey church, and survive in a far more complete state than their southern counterparts (*31*). The completeness of the evidence makes it possible for us to see that there were several phases in their construction, perhaps with pauses of some years between those phases that may have resulted from the financial difficulties in which the abbey was apparently finding itself (see above pp.16-18). There are perhaps also clues that the eventual consequences for the building as a whole of what was being done in the earlier phases were not always fully thought through. As an example of this, although, as has been said, the base course was laid out without a break as far as the stair turret at the north-west corner of the north transept, insufficient allowance was made in doing so for the scale of the clasping pilaster buttress at the north-east corner of the north transept chapel, and the pilaster's width had to be increased at mid-height in

31 Dryburgh Abbey, the north flank of the choir and the east side of the north transept. © *Crown copyright, reproduced courtesy of Historic Scotland*

a rather unusual way, with a mask corbel below a quadrant outward curve (*32*). Similarly, in setting out the outer walls of the aisle and chapel, inadequate thought seems to have been given as to how the stone vaulting over the aisles was to relate to the walls and arcades, and, when the vault was eventually built, adjustments had to be made at a higher point to provide suitable springing points for it (*33*).

The architectural evidence indicates that the external walls which contained the northern choir aisle and transept chapel, and which rose to only a single storey since there was no outer wall to the gallery, were built to full height before the internal arcades that carried the upper storeys. Those outer walls were essentially a continuation of the campaign during which the presbytery was constructed, and the windows which pierced them were smaller versions of the tall windows along the presbytery flanks. The only difference is the addition of a band of dogtooth decoration to the hood moulds, both internally and externally (*34*), except for the interior of the north window of the north transept chapel. Running below the external wall-head cornice is a corbel table of mask corbels.

The details of the chapel walls reflect architectural fashions that slightly pre-date those of the arcades as eventually built; nevertheless, since the responds of those arcades were integral with the walls, they were necessarily built with them. The two responds of the north aisle and chapel are of a slightly later type than the earliest of those on the south side that have already been discussed, at

32 Dryburgh Abbey, the exterior of the north choir and transept chapels. © *Crown copyright, reproduced courtesy of Historic Scotland*

33 Dryburgh Abbey, the vaulting at the junction of the north choir and transept chapels. *Fawcett*

34 Dryburgh Abbey, the window of the north choir chapel. © *Crown copyright, reproduced courtesy of Historic Scotland*

the south end of the transept arcade and at the junction of the south transept chapel and choir aisle walls. This again supports the view that work on the south side where it adjoined the east conventual range was carried out first. However, the eastern responds of the arcades on both south and north sides of the choir appear to have been essentially similar (see *20A*), suggesting that the eastern wall of the south choir aisle was being built around the same time as the presbytery and outer walls of the north aisle and chapel, rather than as part of the very first operations. These responds, which rise from water-holding bases (*35C*), consist of a triplet of shafts, the leading one being keeled, which are set against a pilaster which was itself flanked by disengaged shafts. The respond at the north end of the north transept arcade is rather more complex, and is likely to have been finished a little later: the simple right angles of the pilaster are here replaced by rolls set between hollows and framed by angled fillets (*20C*).

The major pier which supported the north-east angle of the tower, is likely to have been built next, and probably not long after the outer walls of the north choir aisle and transept chapel (*36*). It is composed of triplets of shafts on the cardinal axes, the leading ones being keeled, with pairs of keeled shafts on the diagonal axes. Although this is the only tower pier to survive complete, the

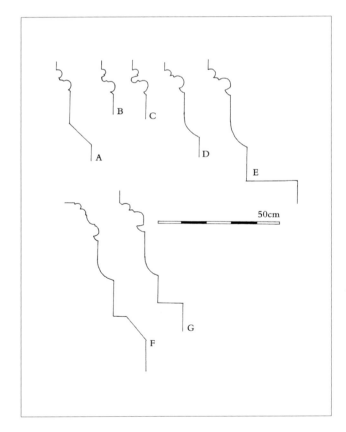

50cm

35 Dryburgh Abbey, measured sections of bases: A. the south respond of the south transept arcade; B. the respond at the junction of the south choir and transept chapels; C. the east responds of the choir arcades; D. the central pier of the north choir arcade; E. the second pier from the crossing of north nave arcade; F. the third and fifth piers from the crossing of the north nave arcade; G. the west respond of the north nave arcade. *Fawcett*

36 Dryburgh Abbey, the north-west crossing pier. *Fawcett*

fragmentary base of the south-east crossing pier shows that was of the same type. The bases of these piers are of similar water-holding form as the north transept respond, while the cap has slight modelling giving the outline of water-leaf forms. By contrast with this tower pier, the intermediate piers of the north choir and transept arcades are of a significantly different type (*37A* and *38*). The sub-bases of these intermediate piers have an intake in the form of a concave flare, and the piers themselves have heavy filleted shafts to the cardinal directions and quarter-shafts to the diagonal directions, the shafts being separated by right-angled spurs; the capitals have bands of horizontal mouldings between the abacus and the necking. These piers have analogies with piers in the crypt and Blackadder Aisle of Glasgow Cathedral (*39*), and in the nave of Inchmahome Priory (*40*),[15] the former probably dating from around the early 1240s, and the latter from after the foundation of 1238. On this basis, the completion of the arcades of the choir and north transept, with the construction of the intermediate piers and the arches they supported, seems unlikely to be earlier than around the end of the second quarter of the thirteenth century.

It should be noted that there are slight but significant changes of design in the arcade arches. On the north side of the choir there are two orders of broad chamfers with a triple roll to the outer order, whereas in the north transept there

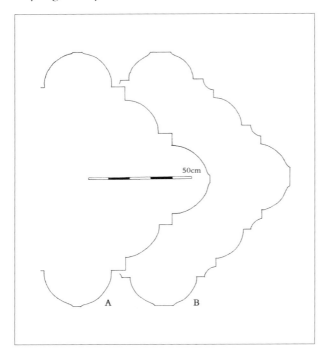

37 Dryburgh Abbey, measured sections of piers: A. the central pier of the north choir arcade; B. the second pier from crossing of the north nave arcade. *Fawcett*

38 Dryburgh Abbey, the central pier of the north choir arcade. *Fawcett*

39 *Above* Glasgow Cathedral, a pier in the crypt. *Fawcett*

40 *Right* Inchmahome Priory, the nave arcade. © *Crown copyright, reproduced courtesy of Historic Scotland*

are three broad chamfers. Since the stub of the south transept arcade arch had two orders of triple rolls and a single broad chamfer, the most likely building sequence for the construction of the arcade arches would seem to be: first, the south transept, followed by the north side of the choir, and then the east side of the north transept. This would again fit with the evidence that the parts of the church next to the east range were built first, and that work then moved to the east end of the main body of the church before moving westward through the outer walls and then the lower storey of the choir and the north transept chapels.

The surviving aisle and chapel on the north side would presumably have been covered not too long after completion of the arcades with the three compartments of quadripartite (four-part) stone vaulting now seen, and these were eventually covered by the lean-to roofs of the gallery. (see 32) The siting of the triplet vaulting shafts in relation the junction of the outer walls of the chapels, which was established when those walls were built, and which was governed by the intended bay rhythm of the arcade piers, was to create a problem when it came to constructing the vaults, since they had been set well back from the angle at the junction of the walls (see 33). To solve this problem, first the upper part of the wall above capital level was set back at an angle of forty-five degrees, and then an additional arch of ribs was provided to connect the shafts, an approach that smacks somewhat of the make-do-and-mend. It can perhaps be argued that the southern chapel was vaulted before its northern counterparts, since its ribs were triple rolls, similar to those in the outer orders of the south transept arcade. By contrast, the north aisle and chapel ribs have hollow chamfers of a similar kind as those which were to be used in the arches of the later bays of the clearstorey (41). The bosses at the centre of each bay of vaulting in the northern aisle and chapel were decorated with fine carving: the outer bays have stiff-leaf foliage of mid-thirteenth-century type, while the central bay has a depiction of Christ in majesty (42). Traces of painted decoration have been found on the vaulting and arcade arches, some with foliage patterns, and others with geometrical designs, though little of this now survives.

There may have been a further short pause before construction of the gallery stage, between the arcade and the clearstorey, and it is worth noting that when it was built its openings were set on a slightly different vertical axis from the arcade arches below them (see 31). We cannot know the reason for this, though it may be suspected that for some reason it was not possible to view the two storeys simultaneously at this stage of the building operations. One reason for this could simply have been that scaffolding was obstructing the view. But is it perhaps even possible that there was a temporary roof above arcade level which allowed the parts of the church that had been completed to be brought into use, but which made precise alignment of the new work difficult? The design of the gallery as built is unique in Scotland. There was clearly no intention that it should be a usable space, since the roof over it sweeps down quite steeply to

41 Right Dryburgh Abbey, the vaulting of the north choir chapel.
© *Crown copyright, reproduced courtesy of Historic Scotland*

42 Below Dryburgh Abbey, the roof boss in the bay at the junction of the north choir and transept chapels.
© *Crown copyright, reproduced courtesy of Historic Scotland*

the outer wall-head of the chapels, and there appears to have been no intention to floor the space above the chapel vaults. Nevertheless, maintenance access was certainly provided, on the south side at least, as can be seen from the doorway that opens off the spiral stair in the corner of the south transept.

The most common way to treat the face of this storey towards the interior would have been to have open arches, as at Glasgow Cathedral (see *28*), or to have blind decorative arcading, as in the north transept at Dundrennan Abbey. For an order that espoused austerity, it could even have been left as blank walling, as is to be seen at the Welsh Cistercian abbey of Tintern.[16] But the approach that was adopted was to have a single cusped circular opening in each bay, which is framed by an arch with continuous mouldings and a depressed two-centred head. In this, the design reflects a wider fashion of the middle decades of the thirteenth century, which saw several leading master masons once again experimenting with circular openings. In the 1240s Westminster Abbey had them in the outer walls of the galleries above the chapels round the eastern chevet and in the transepts, for example (*43*),[17] while Lichfield Cathedral had triangular groupings of them in its nave clearstorey soon afterwards (*44*).[18] In the north transept of Hereford Cathedral, which owes much to Westminster and was started around the 1250s,[19] there are circular windows in both the clearstorey and the gallery outer wall (*45*).

WESTMINSTER ABBEY.
ELEVATION OF THREE EXTERIOR COMPARTMENTS ON THE NORTH SIDE.

43 Westminster Abbey, external elevations. Neale, *Westminbster Abbey*

44 Lichfield Cathedral, the nave. *Fawcett*

While none of these provides precise parallels for the internal circlets of Dryburgh, they do help us to appreciate the wider context for an interest in circular openings at this time. They also remind us – if a reminder were needed – that Scotland's artistic links with England continued to be very strong. But these parallels are of particular value in indicating that this phase of the work is likely to be of around the central decades of the century, and thus some years after the outer walls of the choir aisles and transept chapels, albeit perhaps not so long after the intermediate arcade piers and arches of those chapels.

The top stage of the three-storeyed design of the choir and transepts, the clearstorey, shows a number of sequential changes of design, perhaps linked with further pauses in the operation that resulted from the financial problems in which the abbey was finding itself in the 1240s and 50s (see *26* and *31*). The earliest part of the clearstorey was presumably that over the aisle-less presbytery, but only the end of this survives where it adjoins the aisled choir, and it is possible that it may have been modified to some extent in the later Middle Ages as part of the repairs after English-inflicted damage (*colour plate 5*). Certainly the area below this shows signs of some reconstruction, with the apparent insertion of a blind quatrefoil at gallery level, which necessitated the truncation of the wall shafts below that. But, if the evidence of the surviving fragment of the presbytery

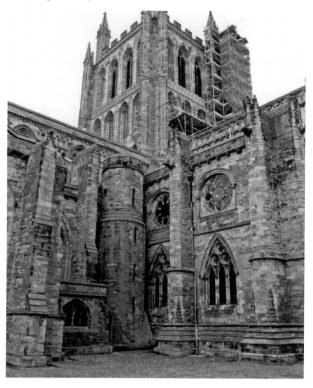

45 Hereford Cathedral, the north transept. *Fawcett*

clearstorey can be trusted, over the presbytery this storey was slightly more squat than it was over the choir and transept chapels.

The clearstorey over the eastern bay of the choir, which was probably built next after the presbytery clearstorey, was slightly wider than that in the other bays, since the bay division was a little to the east of the arcade respond. This bay had five open arches on the inner side of the wall passage; the arches are carried on cylindrical shafts, and there is a wider central arch corresponding to the window on the external wall, flanked on each side by a pair of narrower arches. An opening in the outer wall to the west of the window perhaps gave access to a sanctus bell, the frame of which could have been supported by corbels above the opening. After the east choir bay there was a marked change of design in the clearstory of the bay next to the crossing, where there were just three broad arches on the inner side of the passage. Those arches have trifoliate heads, and are carried on small piers with a leading engaged shaft, rather than on cylindrical shafts. It might be thought that this design was at least partly a result of late medieval rebuilding, since it is so unlike the bay to the east, and there are also some differences from the clearstorey bays in the adjacent transept. However, on balance it is more likely that its design represents an intermediate stage in the mid-thirteenth-century works before the design as seen in the transept clearstorey was eventually finalised.

The two clearstorey bays in the transept also have three arches per bay, the central one being of course wider than the others because of its relationship with the window in the outer wall; the piers are slightly more substantial than those in the west choir bay, and the arches are uncusped (*46*). Despite the changes, there are more significant similarities than differences between the clearstorey designs in the west choir bay and transept, and in each the arches have mouldings of three orders of hollow chamfers. These hollow chamfers, as has been said, show some kinship with the paired hollow chamfers of the chapel vault ribs below. Even more worthy of note, as an indication that they are products of the same extended campaign, however, is the fact that in both the west choir bay and the transept the arches emerge from vertical springer blocks that rise up above the supporting piers.

Springer blocks represent an interesting refinement of detail. They began to be used in a number of English buildings around the second quarter of the thirteenth century,[20] and became more widespread in the middle of the century. In view of the possible parallels that we have seen with Westminster Abbey, in the circular windows at gallery level, it is worth noting that a number of cases of the use of springer blocks are also to be found there. In Scotland possibly the first relatively

46 Dryburgh Abbey, the east side of the north transept.
© *Crown copyright, reproduced courtesy of Historic Scotland*

securely dated examples of this feature are in the choir arcades at Elgin Cathedral, which date from after the fire of 1270 (*47*).[21] The examples at Dryburgh might arguably be a little earlier than that though, in view of the evidence we have considered that points to a relatively protracted building operation, it is perhaps unlikely that they date very much before then. As well as being used in the later clearstorey, springer blocks are also found in the windows of the great front to the main space of the north transept, which, despite being now very damaged, can still be seen to have been a strikingly elegant composition (*48*). There was evidently a grouping of three tall and highly enriched lancet windows at the level corresponding with the arcade and gallery, and an upper level of three – or possibly more – rather more simply treated lancets rising through the level of the clearstorey into the gable. Immediately around the window openings of the lower tier were continuous mouldings with provision for internal glazing frames; embracing those continuous mouldings externally were outer arches carried on pairs of engaged shafts, with bands of dogtooth decoration to the piers between the windows. The high quality of this phase of work is affirmed by the carefully characterised bearded-head corbel supporting the internal hood moulding of the eastern window; this had to be recessed into the masonry of the adjacent wall, which had been built in a slightly earlier phase of work.

47 Elgin Cathedral, the east respond of the south choir arcade. © *Crown copyright, reproduced courtesy of Historic Scotland*

48 Dryburgh Abbey, the north transept gable wall. © *Crown copyright, reproduced courtesy of Historic Scotland*

Perhaps a little perversely, since the lower parts of the south transept were the first part of the church to be built, the upper parts of that transept were probably only brought to completion some years after its northern counterpart. There is unfortunately insufficient of the openings at gallery and clearstorey level of this transept to be able to locate them within the building sequence with any precision, though the simple keeled moulding and square abacus of the window at clearstorey level on the west side of the transept certainly suggest that its jambs had been set in place relatively early within the overall sequence. However, the springer blocks of its rear arch, which relate to those in the north transept clearstorey, indicate that the arch of this window was only built some decades later (*49*); and the great south gable window must be even later in this thirteenth-century building sequence (see *11*). This window rises above the roof of the adjacent dormitory, and has a base that was stepped up around the dormitory roof. It is a simple but highly effective design, with substantial mullions dividing the five lights with pointed-arched heads which press up to the underside of the containing arch. The closest analogies in Scotland for this type of window are probably to be found in the south transept at Pluscarden Abbey,[22] where the comparable – but smaller – window also rises above the roof of the adjacent

49 Dryburgh Abbey, the window fragment on the west side of the south transept. *Fawcett*

dormitory (*50*). On an even smaller scale, comparisons can be made with the nave clearstorey at Sweetheart Abbey (*51*).[23] In both cases it is likely that the windows are of the later years of the thirteenth century, and that is also the most likely dating for the Dryburgh window.

As was said in discussing the presbytery, the high spaces of the eastern arm and transepts were possibly covered by timber barrel ceilings rising from the wall head above the clearstorey. The containing arch of the south transept window, which is of only very slightly pointed form, could well reflect the arched profile of such a ceiling, with the small square window above it lighting the roof space within the ceiling. There is an intake in the masonry over the main window, directly above the likely arch line of the barrel ceiling, which may have been provided as the seating for a collar beam of the roof. None of this is certain, however, and the only high part of the church for which we have firm evidence of the way it was covered over is the area within the central tower, which clearly had stone vaulting since the springing at the north-east survives (see *31*). The vault there sprang from the base of the clearstorey which in fact meant that, although the tower would have risen externally to a greater height than the surrounding arms of the building, as viewed from within the church it would have been covered over at a lower level. On analogy with what we know of

50 Pluscarden Abbey, from the south-west (before restoration of the church). © *Crown copyright, reproduced courtesy of Historic Scotland*

51 Sweetheart Abbey, a nave clearstorey window. *Fawcett*

central towers elsewhere, it was presumably intended that the Dryburgh tower should rise at least a full storey above the surrounding roofs of choir, transepts and nave, and it may have been intended to be capped with a stone or timber and lead spire. Yet, bearing in mind the financial difficulties that the abbey was evidently experiencing, it cannot be ruled out that it was never carried up to its full intended height. Towers were frequently seen as a luxury that could be cut back on when funds were in short supply.

THE NAVE

It has already been suggested above that the south-east processional doorway, in the eastern bay of the nave towards the cloister, was built around the same time as the east conventual range (see *21*), and it is possible that as much as three bays of the outer wall of the south aisle were started as part of the same operation, perhaps as an abuttal section for the choir and tower, and in order to support a length of the north cloister walk roof. Although this wall rose no higher than the aisle, and would have been braced externally by the roof of the cloister walk, it is rather thin even for such a relatively undemanding situation, and it was perhaps because of this that it was decided to have buttresses along a wall that was often left unbuttressed at other churches. However, rather unusually, these buttresses were constructed on the interior of the wall, towards the aisle, rather than on the outside where they would have projected into the cloister walk. One of the

52 Culross Abbey, internal buttressing along south nave wall. *Fawcett*

few other examples of such internal buttressing is in the aisle-less nave of the Cistercian abbey church at Culross,[24] which was built soon after its foundation in 1217 (52). As has been said, on the easternmost of those buttresses there are slight projecting tusks of masonry, which could indicate the line of the original rood screen.

So far as we can judge from the very scant surviving evidence, work on the eastern bays of the nave may have been started soon after the transept arcades had been completed. However, the evidence is extremely fragmentary, and has been rendered even more difficult to interpret because it is clear that much of it had to be rebuilt in the later Middle Ages; there may also have been some modern reconstruction of a number of piers. On the north side, it has been seen

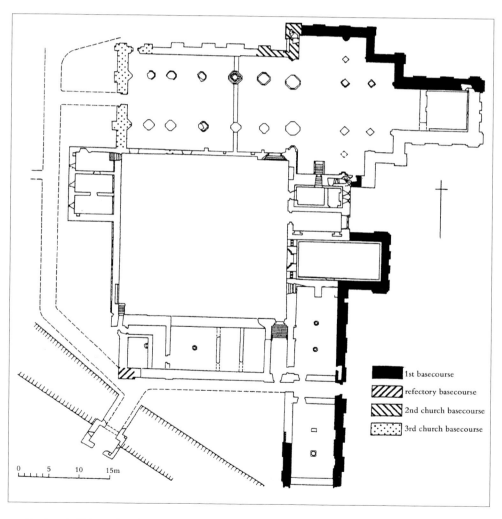

53 Dryburgh Abbey, plan showing the location of base course types. *Sylvia Atevenson/Historic Scotland*

that there is a change of base course at the stair turret at the north-west corner of the north transept (see *17*), and that new base course then continues along at least the first bay of the outer wall of the north aisle, after which it has been destroyed for four bays (*53*). Even where parts remain it is manifestly incomplete, but its main element can be seen to have been a deep chamfer, with a bottom roll, above a chamfer and vertical face (see *15*B, a formation which has parallels in mid-thirteenth-century work at Glasgow Cathedral, for example.[25] However, apart from the south aisle wall, parts of the west front, and some pier fragments, very little survives of the nave (*54*).

Nevertheless, such evidence as there is suggests that there was much rebuilding in the later Middle Ages, and only the stump of the second pier from the crossing on the north side is identifiably of the thirteenth-century operations (*55*). This pier has a base of water-holding form, above a sub-base with a concave flare like that already seen in the intermediate pier on the north side of the choir (see *35*E). Such treatment of sub-bases is characteristic of the central decades of the century, and other examples are to be seen in parts of Elgin Cathedral, Glasgow Cathedral (see *39*),[26] and Paisley Abbey. The pier itself has broadly filled shafts to the cardinal faces, with quarter shafts between hollow chamfers to the diagonal faces. As with the sub-bases, this can probably be best understood as a slightly later development on the type seen in the intermediate piers of the choir

54 Dryburgh Abbey, the remains of the nave. © *Crown copyright, reproduced courtesy of Historic Scotland*

55 Dryburgh Abbey. The second pier from the crossing of the north nave arcade. © *Crown copyright, reproduced courtesy of Historic Scotland*

and transept arcades. Also as with those piers, there are again some parallels with piers at Glasgow Cathedral; in this case the slightly more complex sequence of quarter shafts and concave curves along the flanks show similarities with piers in the ambulatory at Glasgow which, of course, slightly post-date those in the crypt there that were referred to earlier (56). The respond built in with the south aisle wall, at the junction with the transept, also appears to have been remodelled at this time (57). However, nothing of what remains of the rest of the arcade bases appears likely to date from before the later fourteenth century at the earliest, although we shall see that the basic form of the thirteenth-century piers was to be very closely copied in the later work.

One of the many mysteries of Dryburgh is what was the original intention for the length of the nave? It may be that it was never completed as initially intended. It would not be the only Premonstratensian church where this happened; at the Carmarthenshire abbey of Talley (58),[27] for example, highly ambitious plans for an aisled nave of eight bays proved to be unachievable, and a nave of no more than four bays with a single aisle was eventually completed. It may also be noted that at Dryburgh's own mother house of Alnwick the excavators considered there was evidence that the two western bays of the nave represented a later campaign of building.

56 Glasgow Cathedral, an ambulatory pier.
Fawcett

57 Dryburgh Abbey, the pier respond
fragment at the east end of the south nave
wall. *Fawcett*

58 Talley Abbey. *Fawcett*

In the final late medieval arrangement at Dryburgh itself, as has been said, the monastic choir extended down into the nave, and the two eastern bays of the nave were separated from the rest by a screen wall, the pulpitum, the lowest course of which is still to be seen. But even if those two bays had not contained the choir from the start, the construction of their arcade storey would have been required to accommodate the pulpitum and rood screen, and to brace the crossing tower. From the surviving fragments of the arcade bases we can see that those two eastern bays had been given a very similar span to the bays of the choir east of the crossing. The distance from one pier centre to the next is in each case about 4.6m. The two next bays were made rather wider, at around 5.2m. By contrast, the western two bays, which would appear to be an entirely late medieval rebuild, since they had a different base course along the west side and the north side of the west bay, were given an unusually narrow span, at about 3.5m. As we shall see later, there are also indications that there had been thoughts of not rebuilding those two western bays at all. Evidently, the length of the nave as we see it was only fixed at the end of a number of building phases, and as a consequence of more than one change of mind. It should also be said that on plan the nave has a rather disproportionately truncated appearance, and it was certainly shorter in relation to the total length of the building than the nave of its mother house at Alnwick, which had eight bays in its final form.

All of this raises the question as to whether there could have been an initial intention to have a nave longer than the six bays of varying span which is all that we now have evidence for. The only way of refuting or confirming this possibility would be to carry out more complete archaeological investigation than has so far been carried out at the abbey. Nevertheless, in speculating on this possibility there are a number of factors that can be taken into account. One of those hinges on the relationship of the west front with the west conventual range. If, as seems possible, a west range had been intended from the start, even though it was never built, that range would have projected well to the west of the existing late medieval west front of the church. It must be conceded that there is no overwhelming reason why the west front should not have been set back behind the outer face of the west range, since this happens at a number of English houses of the order, including Bayham, Easby and Egglestone. There are, however, two factors which might support the argument that there had been an intention that the nave should be longer than what we now see, and that it was perhaps intended to terminate at a west front on the same line as the outer face of a west range.

In the first place, within and above the north wall of the late medieval block that was eventually built on the west side of the cloister, there is masonry that has indications of being a continuation of the south wall of the nave beyond the line of the existing west front, suggesting that the nave was indeed at one stage in its history intended to extend further west (59). In the second place, it may be worth considering a relatively frequently found geometrical relationship between the cloister and the nave, by which the diagonal of the former equalled the length of the latter.[28] This was presumably one of those relationships that might be almost casually generated in the processes of pegging out medieval complexes with the limited equipment and geometrical knowledge then available, in which swinging one length of rope through forty-five degrees would be an easy way of fixing the diagonal of one and the length of the other. At Dryburgh, if it were assumed that the nave had been intended to extend as far west as a west range that was of the same width as the south range, that would result in the nave having a length that was very similar to the diagonal of the cloister. It might be added that a nave of that length could accommodate eight bays of about the same span as the bays in the choir and the two eastern bays of the nave (60).

It must be conceded that none of this could be regarded as offering firm proof that the nave was intended to be longer than what is now seen. It should also be added that a geophysical survey which was carried out in the area in 2004 was unable to find clear evidence to support the possibility of a greater length having been intended, though it was said that 'a number of high amplitude responses occurring in the time-slices at all depths would certainly suggest that some form of remains exist within the subsurface'.[29] Under the circumstances, perhaps all that can be said is that the notion that there had been initial aspirations for a longer nave cannot be ruled out, and that it remains an attractive subject for further investigation.

59 Dryburgh Abbey, the masonry at the junction of the south and west walls of the nave, as viewed from the north-west. *Fawcett*

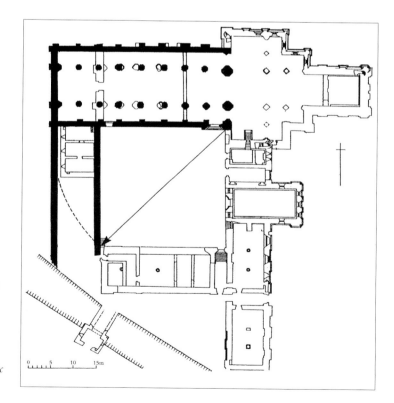

60 Dryburgh Abbey, speculative plan indicating a nave of eight bays, of the same length as the diagonal of the cloister, and with a west range aligned with the west front of the church. *Sylvia Stevenson/Historic Scotland*

LATER MODIFICATIONS TO THE PRESBYTERY AND NAVE

The life of Dryburgh Abbey as an active religious community lasted for 410 years. We can be certain that the form of that life would have undergone modifications of many kinds over such a long period, and we do know that from the early fifteenth century, in particular, there was a tendency to provide increasingly splendid liturgical fixtures and furnishings as the backdrop to growing elaboration in the forms of the daily liturgy, and of the celebration of the mass in particular.[30] Changes of that kind tend to leave relatively few traces in a building that is in a ruined state, though the construction of the wall that cut off the eastern part of the presbytery, and of a later pulpitum across the second nave bay from the east were presumably at least partly generated by such changes in liturgy linked with new fashions in liturgical furnishings.

The principal stimuli for structural changes to the church at late medieval Dryburgh, however, were almost certainly the devastating attacks inflicted on the abbey by English forces in the fourteenth, fifteenth and sixteenth centuries. As we have seen, there were references to damage of a kind that might have affected the structure of the church in 1322, 1385 and 1545, while there was a major but accidental fire in 1443 (see above pp.22,26,35, and 29). The architectural evidence tends to suggest that a significant proportion of the modifications that have left traces of themselves, and that can be approximately dated by comparison with other buildings, were carried out after the attack of 1385. Conversely, it seems unlikely that after the attack of 1545 there was much chance to make significant repairs before the onslaught of the Reformation. Nevertheless, it certainly cannot be assumed that all of the identifiable reconstruction followed the attack of 1385, and some of the works that were necessitated by that attack were probably in any case so long delayed that they belong to entirely distinct operations. In attempting to come to terms with what was done, we shall first look at the changes to the presbytery, and then attempt to unravel what was done to the nave.

The greatest single change in the presbytery which has left any evidence of itself involved the removal of the decorative arcading around the lower wall below the windows (see *25*). But the extent of the damage discernible at this level suggests there would also have been major damage at the higher levels, even if those upper levels are now so completely lost that we cannot know how extensive was the need for repair. Within the area of the eastern part of the presbytery, which was perhaps enclosed by the new cross wall not long after the damage was caused, we see extensive signs of fire damage to the stone. Intriguingly enough, however, there seems to have been no attempt to remove completely the affected wall arcading along the east and south walls, though the edge of the bench below the arcading where it is still visible has at least been chamfered back. The limited nature of the remedial works could suggest that this area was no longer deemed to be of sufficient liturgical importance to justify complete obliteration of the evidence of the destruction, though it could also be that the damaged masonry was hidden from sight in some other way, by timber wainscoting or furnishings, for example.

There was evidently a more carefully contrived attempt to patch up the damaged masonry in the area of the presbytery west of the new cross wall, which is hardly surprising since it had presumably become the setting for the re-located high altar (see 26). On the north side, where the evidence is most complete, it can be seen that the wall was simply cut back where the wall arcading had been, and, although the masonry face that was left was rather rough, once it was plastered over it would have been difficult to see where the arcading had been removed. Above this level there was a need for further work to patch up the masonry. One likely insertion was a blank quatrefoil below the clearstorey, which was presumably intended to continue the themes of the gallery openings further west. There may also have been repairs to the clearstorey, but the evidence here is less certain.

It has to be said that, although the remedial works to the west bay of the presbytery seem to have been more carefully managed than those in the walled-off eastern section, neither gives the impression of having been executed to the most exacting standards. It must also be said that there is nothing in the remedial work on the presbytery that offers firm diagnostic clues as to its date.

By contrast, the work in the nave, which we shall examine next, appears to have been carried out at considerable expense and with a far higher level of care. In view of the difference of quality between the works on the presbytery and the nave, and the fact that the choir bays east of the crossing, between the presbytery and the nave, show relatively few signs of reconstruction, it is probably reasonable to suspect that work on the nave was instigated in response to different circumstances and at a different time. Nevertheless, that is certainly not to suggest that rebuilding of the nave was an entirely homogeneous operation. As indicated above when discussing the original design of the nave, there are definite signs of changes of mind having taken place in the course of rebuilding.

As has already been said, of the original structure of the nave as much as the three eastern bays of the south aisle outer wall may have been retained from the work started at the turn of the twelfth and thirteenth centuries, while on the north side the eastern bay of the mid-thirteenth-century aisle wall also appear to have been at least partly retained. In addition, it has been said that at least the second arcade pier from the east, on the north side was retained from the mid-thirteenth-century work (see 54). Otherwise it appears that the nave must have been extensively rebuilt; what is particularly striking, however, is that considerable efforts were evidently made to match the new work with the old, with the form of the earlier piers being closely copied.

There are strong indications that a decision was taken early in the rebuilding campaign to truncate the nave, leaving it no more than four bays in length. This is to be seen initially in the survival of a section of base course aligned on a north–south axis in the south wall of the nave as seen from the cloister, on the west side of the fourth bay from the east (*61*). Corresponding to that base course internally there is the stump of a returned section of wall which, under the circumstances, is best interpreted as the line of an intended west front. Support for the idea that it was intended to truncate the nave is seen in the cutting of a doorway to the cloister through the aisle wall within the fourth bay (*62*). Such provision of what is now seen as a middle doorway towards the cloister is distinctly unexpected. Considered together with the other evidence, it would be hard to come to any other conclusion than that a doorway was created in this bay on the assumption that there would be no scope for a door further west, because the nave as it was to be rebuilt would not be long enough for it.

By the stage that the nave was being rebuilt, it may be that there was simply felt to be little need for much space to the west of the monastic choir. It is unfortunate that we know less than we would wish about the spatial requirements for lay brethren in Premonstratesnian churches. However, for the churches of an order that took so many of its ideas from the Cistercians, it is probable that, as with the Cistercians, the lay brethren would initially have had a choir that was separate from, and to the west of, the canons' choir. But by the time the nave of Dryburgh was being rebuilt, recruitment of lay brethren is likely to have ceased, with the consequence that there was no requirement to

61 Dryburgh Abbey, the fragment of base course of the same type as that along the west front, embodied within the south wall of the nave. *Fawcett*

62 Dryburgh Abbey, the north and west sides of the cloister. © *Crown copyright, reproduced courtesy of Historic Scotland*

provide a choir for them. Beyond that, since there was no overwhelming need to provide space for the worship of the layfolk of the surrounding communities, it may have been felt that truncating the nave was an acceptable way of saving funds by avoiding the construction of parts for which there was no longer any liturgical need. However, more expansive counsels were soon to prevail. There is unlikely to have been a long period of time before it was decided to give the nave a further two bays, placing the west front on approximately the same line as the west wall of the cloister, even if, as we have discussed, this may not have been the full extent of the originally intended nave.

Although tantalisingly fragmentary, such evidence as there is for the form of the nave as it was rebuilt in the later Middle Ages is most complete in the two western bays. The most prominent element of the base course across the west front, which returned along the north flank of these bays, is the same as that built into the masonry of the fifth bay on the south side of the nave. The lower walling of the west front may therefore quite simply have been bodily relocated two narrow bays westwards. The main element of this base course is a broad ogee curve (see 15C), comparable with that found in the nave of Dunkeld Cathedral, which was started in 1406,[31] or that of around the mid-fifteenth century beneath the rebuilt north transept at Jedburgh Abbey.[32] But at Dryburgh there is the additional top feature of a string course in the form of a keeled moulding below a chamfer; this latter is a direct copy of the string course above the base course around the eastern parts of the building, and there can be no reason to doubt that this was part of an attempt to match the new work with the old.

Even more striking as evidence of a wish to respect the forms of the earlier building is the close replication of the forms of the thirteenth-century nave piers in the respond of the west front. There can be no question that this respond is late medieval, and that it was built at the same time as the west front, since it is carefully coursed in with the masonry of its inner face (63). Yet even the water-holding form of the base of the thirteenth-century pier was copied, though close inspection does reveal that the profile of the bottom roll was slightly modified by being flattened below the curve (see 35G). Elsewhere in the nave, on the evidence of the first and third piers from the west on the north side, the piers were also close copies of their thirteenth-century predecessors. However, the bases in those two surviving fragmentary examples, while following the concave flares of the earlier sub-bases, had moulding profiles that were otherwise more in keeping with current tastes in their rather shallow sequence of rolls and hollows (see 35F). The wish to attune new work to existing fabric that Dryburgh's nave demonstrates was more common in the later Middle Ages than is often

63 Dryburgh Abbey, the west respond of the north nave arcade. © *Crown copyright, reproduced courtesy of Historic Scotland*

appreciated.[33] But in this case it may have been additionally conditioned by the likelihood that as much as possible of the earlier work was being retained, with the new work being carefully tailored around it.

It is difficult to tell from what remains of the western stump of the wall above the north arcade if the internal elevation of the nave was of three or two storeys (*64* and see *54*). By the later Middle Ages two storeys tended to be the preference, galleries being generally out of fashion. However, there are a number of Scottish buildings where galleries were provided, perhaps for particular reasons of prestige or for historical associations, as at Dunkeld Cathedral, Paisley Abbey and Linlithgow St Michael.[34] In view of the evident wish to respect and retain earlier work, the same is perhaps likely to have been the case at Dryburgh. One aspect of the new work that is particularly worthy of note is that, whatever financial restraints the community may have been suffering, the masonry continued to be of the highest-quality polished ashlar and, as with the base course, the other moulded features are carefully detailed and scaled to the building as a whole. The window at the west end of the north aisle, for example, has reveals in the form of a pair of broad hollows framed by angled fillets (*65B*), a formation that has parallels in the rear-arches of windows at Crichton Collegiate Church, which was founded in 1449.

64 Dryburgh Abbey, the nave viewed from the choir. © *Crown copyright, reproduced courtesy of Historic Scotland*

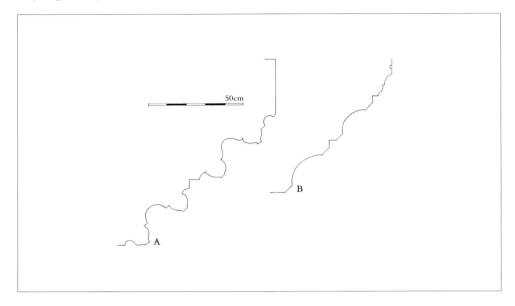

50cm

65 Dryburgh Abbey measured sections of: A. the west doorway jambs and arch; B. the reveal of the window at the west end of the north nave aisle. *Fawcett*

The finest single surviving feature of the new work is the great processional doorway at the centre of the west front (*66*). Like the much simpler new doorways in the south wall of the nave, its head is semi-circular, and is thus a reflection of the revival of arches of this form in Scotland that had been gathering strength from the later years of the fourteenth century, and that is seen at major buildings nearby such as Melrose Abbey. At Dryburgh the doorway has mouldings that rise from deep but shallowly moulded bases, and that run without break around both jambs and arch, with two pairs of filleted rolls framing bands of square flower (*65A*). In the use of multiple filleted rolls and the continuous mouldings, some analogies might be seen with the doorway inserted into the south transept of Melrose Abbey in the early years of the fifteenth century, although in that case the arch is pointed and there is no square-flower decoration between the mouldings (*67*). On the basis of all these parallels, it is most likely that the reconstruction of the western parts of the nave post-dates the 1385 attack, albeit the process of rebuilding is likely to have been relatively extended, and to have involved some significant changes of design.

66 Dryburgh Abbey, the west doorway.
© *Crown copyright, reproduced courtesy of*
Historic Scotland

67 Melrose Abbey, the south transept
doorway. © *Crown copyright, reproduced*
courtesy of Historic Scotland

THE MONASTIC BUILDINGS: THE CLOISTER

As usual, the main nucleus of the monastic buildings was laid out as a series of ranges around an open cloister on the south side of the church (*colour plate 1*), which at Dryburgh was some 27.5m square, and there would have been covered walkways around all four sides of the cloister, both to give sheltered access between the surrounding buildings, and to provide spaces within which a variety of activities could take place (see *9*). The single-pitch roofs of these walks would have been supported on the side towards the open garth by arcade walls, which would probably initially have been open, but may later have been glazed. It may be that the earliest of the cloister arcades were carried on pairs of shafts, and a base that could have formed part of a paired-shaft arcade is preserved in the stone display within the building at the south-west corner of the cloister (*68*).[35] The cloister was a space within which the canons could feel themselves to be apart from the world; indeed, in orders that were more strictly enclosed than the Premonstratensians, the ideal was that the inmates should never have to leave the cloister and the buildings that could be accessed from it. Nevertheless, there were always passageways, or slypes, out of the cloister, sometimes through all three of the surrounding ranges. Those in the east and west ranges could also serve as parlours, where limited conversation might be permitted, but at Dryburgh,

68 Dryburgh Abbey, the fragment of a base possibly from the cloister. *Fawcett*

1 An aerial view from the south–east

2 The transepts

3 The east side of the north transept

4 The doorway from the east cloister walk to the south nave aisle

5 *Left* The choir clearstorey

6 *Below* Painted decoration in the sacristy

7 *Above* The chapter house entrance

8 *Right* Painted decoration in the chapter house

9 The warming house and dormitory

10 The rose window in the refectory west gable

11 The obelisk erected by Lord Buchan

12 The abbey from the south–east

although there is a slype opening off the cloister through the east range, there is no sign that provision was ever made for one on the west side. There was also a passage through the south range, to the east of the refectory undercroft, and in this case the slope of the ground meant that it had to contain a stair down from the level of the cloister.

The doorways into the church and other buildings around the cloister have been discussed when dealing with those buildings, but a number of features belong specifically to the cloister and should be mentioned here. Several of the activities that took place within the shelter of the cloister walks, and especially those in the potentially sunnier south-facing walk on the north side, involved the use of books. The main repository for books was probably a library in the western part of the sacristy chamber, but there was also a book press at the north end of the east wall, adjacent to the library, where books in everyday use might be housed (*69*). This segmental-arched recess has a rebate round the edge for the frame of wooden doors, and slots for two timber shelves. Diagonally opposite that press, in the south-east corner of the cloister, was another recess below a segmental arch, which presumably housed the lavatorium, a basin where the canons washed their hands as a form of ritual cleansing before entering the refectory (see *97*). The stonework surrounding this recess has simple double hollow-chamfered mouldings around it, similar to the later thirteenth-century

69 Dryburgh Abbey, the west side of the east claustral range. © *Crown copyright, reproduced courtesy of Historic Scotland*

mouldings in the north transept clearstorey, and there is a rosette decorating the head of the arch. Above the basin is the springing stone of an arch, which presumably crossed the junction of the west and south cloister walks.

When the east claustral range was started it was intended that the cloister walk in front of it – and presumably the other three walks as well in due course – should be covered by stone vaulting, since there are five vault springings at regular intervals in the more northerly parts of the wall. There is, however, no evidence that the vaulting was ever built, though there is plentiful, if occasionally confusing, evidence that timber roofs were built along the east, north and west sides of the cloister. Along the east side, it seems that the roof rafters rose to a timber wall plate supported by double corbels, and there were further corbels and a string course, presumably where the roof met the wall. A number of pockets set lower in the wall were presumably for the half-collars that must have braced the roof rafters at mid-height. Along the north and west walls are two main levels of pockets with some others at irregular intervals between, perhaps indicating that there were braces which rose up diagonally from the wall to the half-collar, and which would have reflected the angle of the rafters themselves (*70*). Nearer the wall heads there are again double corbels for the wall plate; these survive along the whole of the west side, and at the west end of the north side.

70 Dryburgh Abbey, the north cloister wall. © *Crown copyright, reproduced courtesy of Historic Scotland*

THE EAST CLAUSTRAL RANGE

The range on the east side of the cloister is one of the most complete monastic structures in Scotland, and is of paramount interest for what it can tell us about the planning and architectural forms of such buildings, though some caution has to be exercised since has it undergone major modifications on at least two occasions. As was said in discussing the church, there is an area of slightly rougher masonry in the lower walls of the sacristy and slype, which continues round to the south and east walls of the south transept chapel (see *12* and *13*); since this appears to be earlier than the rest, it is possible that it survives from buildings erected soon after the foundation of the abbey. However, apart from that earlier work, the masonry of the ground-floor and first-floor levels of the rest of the range is strikingly homogeneous. Although construction must have extended over a number of years, and appears to have progressed from north to south at the lower level, there was a clear effort to give the range an architectural unity through the use of ashlar stonework and architectural detailing of a high level of quality.

From the northern flank of the section of the chapter house that projects beyond the body of the range, the same base course runs continuously along the surviving parts of the outward facing east side of the range, and also along the west side of the southern parts of the range that extend beyond the cloister. As already said, this is essentially the same base course as that around the eastern parts of the church, albeit without the two lowest courses of chamfers that were presumably considered essential to scale it to the greater height of the church (see *15*A). One slight difference of detail from the church that may be worth noting is that the windows along the east range were all originally provided with rebates for glazing frames on the outer side of the reveal, whereas in the church they were on the inner side of the reveal. Although this could simply be a reflection of both the relative accessibility and the different functions of the two parts, it is generally true to say that external glazing frame rebates tend to be earlier than internal rebates, and this could be a further reflection of the fact that construction of the church was to be pressed ahead somewhat later than work on the east range. Along the east wall of the range to the south of the chapter house the walls are reinforced by a regular series of pilasters, which are of shallow projection, but which are unusually broad; indeed, they are only a little less broad than the spaces between them. They are capped by paired projecting chamfered courses (*71*).

Because of the sloping ground levels, all of the rooms at the lower level of the range are considerably below the floor of the church, and they step down progressively towards the south, following the fall of the land. As was usual in the lower storeys of conventual ranges, they were all covered by stone vaulting, of either semi-circular barrel form in the northern parts, or of four-part ribbed type in the principal spaces to the south; these vaults supported the floor of the

71 Dryburgh Abbey, the east side of the east claustral range. © *Crown copyright, reproduced courtesy of Historic Scotland*

dormitory above. It is worth noting that considerable efforts have been made to ensure that the vaults all rose to the same level, so that the dormitory floor could be on a single level. Along the lower storey, the sequence of rooms from north to south was: sacristy and library; parlour or slype; chapter house; day stair to the dormitory; warming house; a second slype with a mezzanine chamber above; and a large room, which was perhaps the novitiate (see *9*). At the outer end of the range, and possibly above the water channel which ran nearby, there would have been the undercroft of a latrine or rear-dorter. The whole of the upper floor would have been occupied by the canons' dormitory, apart from the rear-dorter at its southern end. A further storey was added to the range at a later date, but the main physical remains of this are to be seen over the outer part of the chapter house.

The **sacristy**, immediately adjacent to the south transept of the church (*72*), is at a level well below that of the church, and it is also slightly below the level of the cloister. It is a barrel-vaulted rectangular chamber that can be entered in three ways: from a spiral stair leading off the transept at its north-east corner, from a doorway within the main body of the transept, and from a large doorway in its west wall off the cloister (see *11*). However, the second of these has had its head raised at a later stage: the masonry around it is extensively rebuilt, and the

72 Dryburgh Abbey, the sacristy
interior. © *Crown copyright, reproduced
courtesy of Historic Scotland*

present lintel is an up-turned re-used lintel that is unlikely to be earlier than the
sixteenth century. The door towards the cloister is a relatively simple opening of
two orders framed by a hood moulding (see *69*). The only windows are in the east
wall, and are in the form of a grouping of two narrow round-arched openings
below a central vesica (an almond-shaped opening). Internally the windows are
deeply splayed, but externally they are set within larger arches framed by hood
mouldings that extend upwards from a string course at the height of the window
arches. The vesica is framed by similar mouldings, and to its north a higher string
course steps up to the level of the dormitory window sills (*73*). In all of this there
could be parallels with the buildings of the English Cistercians, as seen in the
window groupings of the transept chapels at Fountains Abbey (*74*),[36] or the south
transept gable at Abbey Dore (*75*),[37] and we are again reminded of the continuing
impact of Cistercian attitudes on the Premonstratensians.

The ashlar-built barrel vault rises from a prominent string course that has a
flat upper surface and a broad lower chamfer. Rather curiously, the head of the
vault does not rise quite enough to clear the apex of the vesica. The chamber
was probably originally subdivided by a timber partition, of which no traces
remain. In the eastern part, which would have been the sacristy proper, the
priests would have prepared themselves to celebrate mass at the altars in the

73 Dryburgh Abbey, the sacristy windows. © *Crown copyright, reproduced courtesy of Historic Scotland*

74 Fountains Abbey, the south transept. *Fawcett*

75 Abbey Dore, viewed from the south. *Fawcett*

church, and some of the vestments and other items required at the service
would have been stored here. The western part of the chamber, which would
have been directly accessible from the cloister, probably housed the library,
where the abbey's main collection of books was stored. We are reminded of
the relative importance of the sacristy in the hierarchy of monastic buildings
by the traces of painted decoration that survive. The walls would initially have
been plastered and lime-washed, and on top of this was simple geometrical
decoration, mainly in shades of red and black, which is now best seen at the
eastern end of the string course on the south side (*colour plate 6*). There are traces
of painted masonry lining on the east wall.

The importance of the room is even more clearly demonstrated by the fact
that it had an altar below the windows in the east wall, and it appears to have
been the base of that altar which was heightened and re-used as part of the
memorial to the wife of the eleventh earl of Buchan, who died in 1819. Portrait
medallions of the earl and his countess were set into the raised portion of the
altar, and an obelisk and urn were placed on it, between the windows. The altar
does not seem initially to have been raised above the general floor level, but at a
later stage the floor of the eastern part of the chamber was elevated by two steps
to form a footpace for the altar, although no attempt was made to modify the
benches that ran along the north and south walls in the process.

Associated with the altar was a piscina basin within an arched recess in the south wall, and set into the floor below it is a very rare example of a floor piscina, which had to be re-set when the floor level was raised. The main purpose of the mural piscina was to provide a basin where the vessels used at mass could be washed, and where the celebrating priest could ritually cleanse the hands that were to handle the sacred elements. It is possible that a piscina in the sacristy was also intended to be used for cleansing the vessels used at some of those altars in the church that did not have their own piscinae. The function of the floor piscina is less certain, and its rarity suggests that it was not something that was felt to be widely necessary. One possibility which has been suggested is that any dust on the surface of the wine that was to be consecrated during the mass might be flicked off into such floor drains before the service, since dust would have polluted the liquid that was believed to become the blood of Christ through transubstantiation.[38]

The sacristy now contains a number of monuments to members of the earl of Buchan's family. Most prominent of these is the table tomb to the earl himself, in the middle of the floor, which has a cast of his death mask together with what appear to be astrological calculations and predictions.

The **parlour** or **slype** is to the south of the sacristy and is on the same level as the cloister; like the sacristy, it is covered by an ashlar barrel vault rising from a strongly marked string course (*76*). This room was essentially a passageway from the cloister to the open area of the precinct on its east side, but it had an added function because within its walls essential conversation was permitted between the canons that might have been regarded as inappropriate within the cloister itself. It originally had round-arched openings closed by doors at both ends, those arches rising to a considerably greater height than the doorway from the cloister into the library and sacristy (see *69*). There were two mural aumbries with rebates for wooden door frames built into its south wall. In the nineteenth century it was converted into a second burial vault for members of the Erskine family, as part of which a smaller doorway was inserted in the arch towards the cloister, and the eastern arch was filled by a wall pierced by a pair of large round-arched windows.

The **chapter house**, the second most important in the hierarchy of monastic buildings, was to the south of the parlour (see *69*). It was the main meeting room of the community, where a chapter of the rule by which the canons lived was read on a daily basis, where the community's business was discussed, and where the members of the community confessed their faults and had tasks allocated to them. This long rectangular barrel-vaulted room (*77*), which was of about the same width as the main body of the east range but ran at ninety degrees to it, projected for almost half of its length beyond the range. It was set well below the level of the cloister, and this had the twin advantages of allowing it to have greater height than was possible in the rooms to its north, while the vault still did not break through the level of the dormitory floor above.

76 *Right* Dryburgh Abbey, the parlour or slype. © *Crown copyright, reproduced courtesy of Historic Scotland*

77 *Below* Dryburgh Abbey, the chapter house interior. © *Crown copyright, reproduced courtesy of Historic Scotland*

The entrance from the cloister was given great prominence by means of a combination of elements that had become relatively standardised for chapter houses from well before the later twelfth century, in which the centrally placed doorway is flanked by a pair of subdivided openings (*colour plate 7*). At Dryburgh the doorway would have been given added emphasis if the intended stone vaulting for the east cloister walk had been built, since the arched head would have been very closely framed by a bay of the vaulting. As a piece of design, the door is closely related to the processional doorway into the nave from the east cloister walk. The innermost order similarly has two bands of large dogtooth set in hollows at ninety degrees to each other, but in the chapter house doorway there are no caps to mark a break at the junction of the jambs and arch of this order. As with the processional doorway, there are three outer orders, and the free-standing shafts in the jambs are similarly set against an angled plane of wall (*78*). The caps carried by those shafts are elegantly simple variants of water-leaf forms, the leaves spreading widely beneath the slender rectangular abaci. The openings flanking the doorway are subdivided by two pointed arches supported by three pairs of shafts with capitals of chalice form (*79*). One wonders if the paired shafts which support the sub-arches could have been intended to reflect the forms of the cloister arcade shafts.

78 Dryburgh Abbey, the north capitals of the chapter house doorway. © *Crown copyright, reproduced courtesy of Historic Scotland*

79 Dryburgh Abbey, one of the openings flanking the doorway of the chapter house. © *Crown copyright, reproduced courtesy of Historic Scotland*

The east gable wall of the chapter house, which projects well beyond the main body of the range, is a noble piece of architectural composition (*80*). Its angles are given strong emphasis by paired broad pilasters separated by an engaged three-quarter shaft. Although the upper part of the wall has been extensively rebuilt and heightened, these pilasters clearly rose well above the general wall-head, and would presumably always have been capped by substantial pinnacles, though it is not clear if the large octagonal pinnacle stumps still to be seen are of the original design. Unlike the windows in the rest of the range, those in the projecting part of the chapter house have pointed arches with deep external splays; there is a single window in each flank, and a triplet in echelon in the east wall. The heads of all of these are framed by hood mouldings which rise up from a string course, and on the east gable this string course steps up and down across the narrow pilasters between the windows. These pointed windows are perhaps the earliest of their type to have been used at Dryburgh, and, although round-arched windows continued to be used elsewhere in the range, the use of such arches in the chapter house was perhaps one way of emphasising its importance. While it would be misleading to overstate the architectural influence of the Cistercians on the Premonstratensians, both the overall design of this front and

80 Dryburgh Abbey, the chapter house from the south-east. © *Crown copyright, reproduced courtesy of Historic Scotland*

the relatively early use of pointed arches do appear to echo the approach seen in many Cistercian buildings, as do the water-leaf and chalice caps of the entrance front and the grouping of the sacristy windows.

Internally, the cavernous space and simple geometrical forms of the chapter house are enormously impressive. This impression is enhanced by the high entrance point, well above floor level, which presumably meant that there had to be a stair on the line of the modern timber stair. It may be that this stair was carried on the extrados of a quadrant arch, since there is no break in the stone bench that runs around all four sides of the room, and there would have had to be a break if the stair had a solid support. As in the sacristy and parlour, the vault springs from a strongly marked string course, but in this case the curve of the vault is penetrated by lateral intersections over the windows in the side walls, and the sloping sills of those windows break through the string course. The chamber is of relatively wide span for a semi-circular barrel vault; as in the sacristy, it does not fully clear the rear-arches of the eastern windows.

For their chapter meetings the canons would have sat on the stone benches around the walls, and greater prominence was given to the seats for the abbot and senior obedientiaries along the east wall by a band of decorative intersecting arcading (*81*). It is a possibility that this arcading represents a slight afterthought. The chalice capitals differ from those in the openings flanking the entrance

81 Dryburgh Abbey, the decorative blind arcading in the chapter house. © *Crown copyright, reproduced courtesy of Historic Scotland*

in having rounded rather than square abaci, though that is not necessarily significant. However, it may also be noted that there is a slight break in the curvature of the arcading above the first course, as if there had been some difficulty in installing the arches. Nevertheless, there seems little doubt that, even if it was an augmentation of the original proposals, this was done while construction was still in progress. Such intersecting arcading had perhaps been first used in Scotland in the central decades of the twelfth century, as at Kirkwall Cathedral and Leuchars Parish Church, but it was still in vogue in the last years of the century, as in the north nave aisle of Holyrood Abbey (*82*).[39]

The interior of the chapter house was richly painted.[40] Over a coat of plaster, much of the wall face was decorated with a masonry pattern, which was both incised and picked out in black lines, and there was some additional use of red. Beyond this, the main architectural features were emphasised by patterns of various kinds, with bands of geometrical forms around the edges of the vaulting intersections and windows, and there were painted crosses, diaper patterns and other motifs within the arches of the blind arcading along the east wall (*83* and colour plate *8*). But the most ambitious part of the painted scheme was *trompe l'oeil* intersecting blind arcading along the side walls, which reflected the design of the three-dimensional arcading along the east wall. However, evidence has

82 Above Holyrood Abbey, the decorative blind arcading in the north nave aisle. © *Crown copyright, reproduced courtesy of Historic Scotland*

83 Left Dryburgh Abbey, painting within the arches of the blind arcading in the chapter house. © *Crown copyright, reproduced courtesy of Historic Scotland*

been found which strongly suggests that, at a later date, the painted arcading along the side walls was replaced by timber arcading.

South of the chapter house, a tall round-arched doorway off the cloister gave access to the **day stair** to the dormitory, the door itself being hung within a rebate four or five steps up, and well into the thickness of the wall, since the door had to open towards the cloister (*84*). Beyond the wall thickness the stair was carried on a pair of arches: there is a segmental arch below the lower part of the flight (which could give some idea of how the chapter house stair was carried), and a semi-circular arch below the upper part (*85*). The arches and the piers that carried the stair projected into the space of the warming room, though the stair itself would presumably have been cut off from the room by a thin wall rising from the arches. Despite the fact that the evidence for this stair has been unusually well preserved, it has been confused because at some unknown date, either before or after the Reformation, the upper part of the stair was suppressed to permit construction of another stair that gave access to the upper floor from the east side of the range.

In the earlier days of the Premonstratensian order, when the rule was particularly rigidly followed, the **warming house** contained the one fireplace at which the canons were allowed to warm themselves in the winter months. Later

84 Dryburgh Abbey, the doorway from the cloister to the day stair. © *Crown copyright, reproduced courtesy of Historic Scotland*

85 Dryburgh Abbey, the warming house, looking towards the arches of the day stair. © *Crown copyright, reproduced courtesy of Historic Scotland*

it became what might now be thought of as a common room. It can be entered either from the adjacent outer slype, or from the passage that ran between the east range and the refectory; the head of the door from that passage has been rebuilt at some stage. In the south-east corner of the room was a narrow mural stair that led up to a small mezzanine chamber above the outer slype, the stonework around which has been extensively rebuilt. Being next to the warming house this small chamber was presumably a warm and dry space. It may have been used as a treasury for the storage of the abbey's more precious possessions, and for the documents by which the abbey was able to establish its rights to its estates and privileges. It was lit by a narrow slit window.

The warming house itself is three bays long from north to south, and two bays wide, and was covered by ribbed four-part vaulting carried on two piers along the north–south axis. These piers, of which the bases are no longer evident, were of basically octagonal form, the diagonal faces being shorter than the cardinal faces, and with deep grooves between the faces (*86*). This is a variant on a type of pier that was used in the conventual range undercrofts of a number of Cistercian abbeys, including the west range of Fountains in Yorkshire as completed in the late twelfth-century (*87*),[41] and the chapter house vestibule of Margam in Glamorganshire of the early years of the thirteenth century.[42] In those cases it

86 Dryburgh Abbey, the fragment of a pier in the warming house. *Fawcett*

87 Fountains Abbey, the west range. *Fawcett*

can be seen that it was the profile of the vaulting ribs that governed the form of the piers, and the ribs emerge without any break from the faces of the piers; it is possible this also happened in the Dryburgh warming house. Along the walls the vaulting rose from slender triplets of shafts (*88*). The capitals of these shafts were either decorated with foliage or had groupings of bracket-like projections; the latter are perhaps a simplified version of a type of corbel with three volute-like sprigs seen at some of the northern English Cistercian houses, including Byland Abbey. The room was initially lit by two round-headed windows through its east wall, between which was the fireplace.

It cannot have been a very light room as first built, and at a later stage, possibly after the English attack of 1385, the opportunity was taken to carry out an extensive remodelling. The fireplace in the east wall was replaced by a possibly larger one in the facing west wall, which appears to have had a canopied head flanked by foliage-decorated corbels on which lights could be placed. At the same time, in the east wall, two large new Y-traceried windows with steeply pointed arches and transoms at mid-height were inserted (see *71*). This involved considerable rebuilding, since the southern of the two was placed where the fireplace had been. The other was set slightly to the north of the original northern window, leaving traces of that window to one side, although

88 Dryburgh Abbey, the warming house wall shafts and instered fireplace. © *Crown copyright, reproduced courtesy of Historic Scotland*

this involved extending the window opening across and possibly beyond the pilaster within which – rather unusually – the original window had been set. The southern of the two original window openings was retained, perhaps because it was too close to the stair to the mezzanine chamber to be replaced by one of the new larger windows, although it was enlarged and the hood moulding around its head was removed. There are also traces of a lower arched opening of uncertain use to be seen below it internally. The rather botched appearance that the external east face of the warming house now has may not all date from this phase of works, however, since there were further works when the new, and partly external, stair was formed on this side.

South of the warming house was a second, **outer slype**, or passage. A passage in this position was a not uncommon feature of monastic planning, as may be seen at the Augustinian houses of St Andrews and inchcolm. Since the east range at Dryburgh appears to have extended across the water channel, this passage had the advantage of making it possible to pass from the west and south sides of the claustral complex to the east side without crossing that channel. From within the passage there was also access to the warming house on the north and to the novitiate on the south, and there are intersections in the barrel vaulting that covers the passage around the heads of these doorways.

South of the slype was a room of almost identical proportions and size as the warming room, which was perhaps the space set aside as a **novitiate**, for those who were aspiring to become professed canons (*89*). This room would have been well suited to that use since it was slightly apart from the main claustral complex and the daily life of the community. Indeed, at some houses the wish to have the novitiate beyond the cloister could mean that it was located in the undercroft of the latrine, a location that would not have been as unpleasant as might sound, since the drain would have been separated from the novitiate by solid masonry walls. Although now in a very fragmentary condition, it can still be seen that this room must have been an even more attractive space than the warming house. It had the same type of vaulting and an essentially similar type of pier, although in this case, if the pier has been reconstructed correctly, it had both a base and a capital, the latter of simple water-leaf form. It also had a fireplace towards the southern end of the east wall. In addition, it had the advantage of being able to have more light, since it could have windows on both the east and west sides. It may be noted that the surviving eastward-facing windows have the same saw-tooth chevron decoration around their heads as the doorway to the stair in the southern transept chapel (*90* and see *18*), and it is unlikely that they were far apart from each other in date.

The east range clearly extended yet further to the south (see *9*), beyond the novitiate, and since it seems that the outer part of the range must have crossed the channel which brought a supply of water to the abbey from the Tweed, it is likely that there would have been the canons' **latrine**, known as the rear-dorter or necessary house, on the upper floor, with direct access from the dormitory.

89 Left Dryburgh Abbey, the reconstructed pier in the novitiate. *Fawcett*

90 Below Dryburgh Abbey, the east windows of the novitiate. *Fawcett*

The **dormitory** on the first floor of the east range would have run almost the full length of the range, with the latrine at its outer end (*colour plate 9* and see *93*). The two principal means of access to it were by the night stair from the south transept, and the day stair from the cloister; but there was also access from the spiral stair in the south-east corner of the transept. Initially it would have been an undivided space in which all members of the community were expected to take their rest together, with the abbot at the end closest to the church. But, perhaps as early as the thirteenth century, and despite initial strictures on private space, it is likely that the dormitory would have been subdivided by timber partitions or curtains into two rows of separate cubicles, with a central corridor between. Beyond that, the need for the abbot to exercise hospitality, and to meet the demands that the wider world would place on someone who was also head of a great land-holding corporation, would mean that it would be less disruptive for him to have separate accommodation, away from the dormitory. By the later Middle Ages that accommodation may have been a substantial semi-independent dwelling, though it is not known where it was at Dryburgh.

The dormitory was clearly built along with the immediately adjacent part of the south transept, as can be seen most obviously in the provision of a roof moulding on the south side of the transept gable, as well as in the way that the base of the window above it is stepped up above that moulding (see *93*). The contemporaneity of the two parts is particularly evident in the way that, on

91 Dryburgh Abbey, the junction of the south transept and east claustral range. © *Crown copyright, reproduced courtesy of Historic Scotland*

the west side, towards the cloister, the surviving fragment of the northernmost dormitory window runs into the masonry of the transept and is coursed without break across the junction (*91*). This window is framed by two orders of chamfers, a treatment closely related to that of the adjacent larger window of the transept, though the dormitory window has no hood moulding. Further confirmation that the two parts are coeval is seen in the way that the wall-head corbel table of the dormitory extends northwards into the transept wall, with the outermost chamfer of the transept window reveal rising from it. This corbel table takes the form of a series of moulded corbels carrying a cornice with pellet decoration.

On the opposite, east, side of the dormitory, south of the chapter house, we have what is the most complete evidence in Scotland for the external form that dormitories might be given (*92* and see *71*), other than that at the structurally complete but atypical example at Inchcolm Abbey. The windows are framed by wide round-headed arches with chamfered reveals and no hood moulds, and the sill level of which is marked by a heavy chamfered string course. The original window openings within the containing arches are quite small and have provision for external glazing frames, although many of them were subsequently replaced by even smaller ogee-headed openings, presumably at some stage after the fire of 1385. Many of the corbels of the corbel table survive along what

92 Dryburgh Abbey, the dormitory windows. © *Crown copyright, reproduced courtesy of Historic Scotland*

was the wall-head, albeit nothing of the cornice that they carried. Along the wall above the site of the original warming house fireplace is a short stretch of continuous corbelling which may have supported a chimney stack, though it is likely this represents a later modification.

THE LATER HEIGHTENING AND REMODELLING OF THE EAST CONVENTUAL RANGE

The most intriguing feature of the east conventual range at Dryburgh is that in its final state it had a second floor above the dormitory. Such evidence as there is points to the strong likelihood that this upper floor was not an original feature of the range, but from the little we can understand of it, it does appear to have been of medieval date. It was perhaps part of a campaign of works that also included the remodelling of the windows to the warming house and dormitory that has been referred to above. It is unknown what function this upper floor served, particularly since such upper floors are very unusual and there is little with which to compare it. One other example which might be cited is at the French royal Cistercian abbey of Royaumont, on the outskirts of Paris, and there it is likely quite simply to have been the large numbers of monks that made this additional storey necessary; there cannot have been such a need at Dryburgh, however. Perhaps it could instead have been intended to accommodate some of the functions that might have been housed in the range of the west side of the cloister at other abbeys, a range which appears never to have been built at Dryburgh. Yet it is difficult to imagine that either the abbot or the cellarer would have found it convenient to be placed on an upper storey above the dormitory in this way since it would have been insufficiently prestigious for the former and rather inconvenient for the latter.

A more plausible interpretation might be that the upper storey was added to allow each of the canons to have individual chambers, at a time when some degree of comfort and privacy was no longer regarded as such an unacceptable aspiration as had initially been the case. Unfortunately, the almost complete loss of the added storey, and the fact that further changes were made perhaps both before and after the Reformation, when the range as a whole is thought to have been adapted as a residence for the commendators of the abbey, means that we are on very uncertain grounds in attempting to understand the limited evidence we have.

The chief evidence for the form of the range in its heightened state is pictorial, and that is the views of the abbey in John Slezer's *Theatrum Scotiae* of 1693, by which time the upper storey was already in a state of advanced ruination (see *104* and *105*). Although this evidence must be treated with considerable caution, these views do appear to show that the windows on the side towards the cloister broadly followed the lead of the dormitory windows on the floor below, though the spacing is shown as different, and smaller quatrefoiled openings are depicted between pairs of window heads.

But there are in addition a number of pieces of, admittedly highly enigmatic, architectural evidence for the heightening and remodelling. In the outer face of the south transept gable, an opening from the west clearstorey wall passage, which presumably initially led out onto the wall-head guttering of the original dormitory, was blocked but extended upwards to create a higher opening (*93*). There is also evidence to be seen in the great window of the gable wall. In that window the upper parts of the lights had glazing chases cut into them at some stage, suggesting that the lower part of the window had been blocked by that stage, and that only the topmost portion needed to be adapted for new glazing that was to be set directly into the mullions rather than held by frames. The extent of the glazing chases points to the added upper floor having initially had a relatively flat roof, above which the upper part of the transept gable window could still be glazed. At a later date, however, the window was evidently fully blocked, as can be seen from a number of early views of the abbey, including those of Slezer.

93 Dryburgh Abbey, the face of the south transept gable wall towards the dormitory. © *Crown copyright, reproduced courtesy of Historic Scotland*

The addition of an upper storey to the part of the chapter house that projected beyond the main body of the range was presumably another element of this phase of works (*94*), though it is doubtful that it can ever have risen to the same height as the main body of the enlarged range. The heightened part of the chapter house is of added interest, since it has one of the few features of potential diagnostic significance. That feature is a shoulder-lintelled doorway to a stair turret that was created at the angle above the north-east corner of the chapter house (*95*). In English contexts such doorways, which are sometimes referred to as 'Caernarvon arches', became relatively common in the later thirteenth century, but continued in use for about a century after then. One firmly dated Scottish parallel is to be seen in the refectory of Dunfermline Abbey, to which donations were being made in 1329. This could suggest that the work at Dryburgh had been prompted by the English attack of 1322.[43] A similar date might also be thought possible for the ogee-headed insets in the dormitory windows. However, in the context of the troubled fourteenth century in Scotland, such features can be considerably later than would be expected on the basis of English analogies. At Mugdock Castle in Stirlingshire, for example, very similar ogee-headed windows are found

94 Dryburgh Abbey, the east face of the chapter house.
© *Crown copyright, reproduced courtesy of Historic Scotland*

95 The interior of the added upper storey of the chapter house. © *Crown copyright, reproduced courtesy of Historic Scotland*

alongside shoulder-lintelled doorways in works that are likely to be as late as the 1370s.[44] On this basis, it may be safer to date this work at Dryburgh to after the attack of 1385.

From the limited indications we have for the modified planning of the upper storeys at first-floor level, we can see that a corridor was created along the west side of the range. Small chambers opened off it above the eastern parts of the sacristy and parlour, while the area above the chapter house, beyond the western corridor, appears to have been divided by at least two cross walls incorporating relieving arches that reduced the weight carried by the barrel vault below.[45] Throughout, there was ample provision for large fireplaces. What happened at first-floor level above the warming house and novitiate is no longer clear (*colour plate 9*, and there is no evidence at all for the planning of the added third storey.

It seems there may have been a gallery projecting from the east wall of the added upper storey of the chapter house, since there is what appears to be the seating for a horizontal roof line at the base of the gable itself, below which are corbels which were presumably intended to support a timber wall plate (see *94*). At a lower level shallow pockets have been cut for joists, and the heads of the buttresses between the windows were removed down to that level; between them there may have been a doorway, which was later adapted as a window. Adjacent to the south side of the chapter house at some stage a doorway was cut through the wall of the warming house, and a stair was constructed to give access to the upper floor of the chapter house; this was within the narrow space that had originally been provided for the day stair from the cloister to the dormitory (96). The lower part of the new stair must have extended out against the south flank of the chapter house, and the evidence of a horizontal moulding in the warming room wall, together with sloping chases cut into the chapter house wall, show that there would have been a sloping roof over the outer part of this stair. Presumably the underlying aim in forming this stair was to provide a way of reaching the upper floor without the need to pass through the cloister.

This stair may have been an element in a further stage of modifications that is most likely to date from around the first half of the sixteenth century. The chief diagnostic indicator for the date of this later work is to be seen in rectangular windows with carefully moulded reveals that were inserted into the east and south walls of the upper floor of the chapter house (see *80* and *94*). The remains of two fireplaces in the cross walls above the chapter house might also be part of this campaign, rather than part of the earlier work. At the lower level, in the chapter house itself, at some stage a doorway was cut through the south wall, giving access

96 Dryburgh Abbey, the reversed stair inserted on the site of the day stair. *Fawcett*

both to the warming house and to the area east of the range; this was eventually blocked up in the twentieth century, after the abbey was placed in state care. Most of these later modifications are generally assumed to belong to an operation to adapt this part of the east range as a residence for the commendators, by which time the remaining canons may well have had more comfortable quarters elsewhere. These were possibly in the infirmary, where they could live under a more relaxed regime without breaching the letter of the rule. Perhaps the work dates from the time of Commendator James Stewart (1523-39) (see p.33), who may be assumed to have undertaken some building works, since a stone with arms thought to be his has been re-set in the south-west corner of the cloister (see *101*). Alternatively, the later modifications could date from after the time that the commendatorship was acquired by the Erskine family in 1541, and if that is the case they may post-date the English attacks of the 1540s.

However, these later adaptations appear not to have enjoyed a very long life of high quality occupation. At some stage, within perhaps less than a century after the Reformation, the upper storeys – both the area of the original dormitory on the first floor and the added upper floor – were largely abandoned, and roofs were set down within the walls, immediately above the ground-floor vaults. The traces of these roofs are still to be seen over the sacristy and chapter house (see *95*). This was probably the state of affairs as early as Slezer's 1693 view, in which only portions of the range still had roofs rising above the wall-heads (see *105*).

THE REFECTORY RANGE

The south conventual range was almost completely given over to the refectory, the third most important room in any abbey after the church and chapter house. It was probably built at a slightly later date than the east range, since a fragment of base course towards the west end of the south wall is of a different type from that below the east conventual range and the eastern parts of the church (see *53*). Refectories were frequently raised either a full or part storey above the cloister; this was possibly as a reminder of the upper room in which Christ took his Last Supper with the disciples on the eve of his Passion, but also because a location at first-floor level was an expression of prestige. At Dryburgh the refectory was elevated above a vaulted basement, though, because of the fall of the land, the floor level was less than a full storey above that of the cloister (*97*). It was presumably entered from the cloister towards its west end, close to where the lavatorium recess is to be seen on the west side of the cloister, though nothing survives to indicate the precise position of the doorway, largely because much of the masonry in this area is a modern rebuilding.

The basement was originally divided into two compartments, the eastern part being of four bays of two aisles, and the western part being of two bays of two aisles. Both compartments were covered by ribbed four-part vaulting

97 Dryburgh Abbey, the west wall of
the refectory from the cloister.
© *Crown copyright, reproduced courtesy
of Historic Scotland*

that was carried on piers like those in the warming house and novitiate, in
being of basically octagonal form, but with shorter diagonal faces, and with
the angles deeply quirked (see *86* and *89*). At the east end of the refectory,
where it adjoined the east range, was a covered stairway leading down from the
cloister to the open area between the south range and the water channel (*98*).
This doorway could be barred from the cloister side, and the slot for the bar
can be seen where the facing stone has been lost. The passage containing this
stair was probably intended to be vaulted; it may be that the original design
included a sloping barrel vault rising from the string course that runs parallel
with the slope of the stairs, though there is no evidence that such a vault was
ever built. The stair would probably have been below the dais for the high table
at which the abbot, the principal obedientiaries (office holders of the abbey)
and their guests would sit, but re-facing of the wall at some stage has destroyed
any evidence of the floor line. On the wall above the site of the dais there are
two shallow pockets in the masonry that might conceivably have been intended
to support a canopy of honour over those who were eating at the high table.
It might be mentioned in support of this notion that there are traces of such
a canopy in the side walls of the structurally complete refectory at Inchcolm
Abbey, in the form of marks where the quadrant curve of that canopy abutted
the walls.[46]

98 Dryburgh Abbey, the refectory undercroft. © *Crown copyright, reproduced courtesy of Historic Scotland*

West of the refectory were the kitchens, of which little remains apart from indications of the access into them, and of the roofs where they adjoined the refectory (*99*). A doorway through the west wall of the refectory was the only direct access into the kitchens, and next to it is a small mural aumbry, perhaps for the storage of napkins (see *97*). The doorway is round-arched towards the west, but had a segmental-arched rear-arch towards the refectory. It is likely that, as in the halls of aristocratic residences, there would have been a screened-off vestibule at the entrance end of the refectory. On the outer face of the refectory's west wall there is a short horizontal drip moulding above the doorway, with corbels to support a timber wall plate below it, which suggests that there used to be a flat or lean-to roof over a structure that presumably connected refectory and kitchen. However, this was superseded by a single-storey range with a double-pitched roof that abutted directly against the west side of the refectory. Nothing is known of the plan or form of this building, and it may have been a post-Reformation addition. Slezer shows what appears to be a gabled building directly to the south of the west refectory gable, though it is probable that this is an inaccurate representation of the nearby gatehouse (see *107*).

The refectory range has been extensively modified on at least one occasion, presumably in the course of repairs after one of the fires suffered by the abbey.

99 Dryburgh Abbey, the west wall of the refectory from the west. © *Crown copyright, reproduced courtesy of Historic Scotland*

As part of these works the basement vaults appear to have been reconstructed as a series of barrel vaults rather than four-part vaults (see *98*). For reasons that may be as much financial as structural, many late medieval masons in Scotland appear to have preferred barrel vaults to four-part vaults, and similar replacements are to be seen in undercrofts at the abbeys of Culross and Dunfermline. It is likely that the refectory hall itself was also extensively rebuilt, although, since little more than the east and west gable walls now survive we cannot be certain of this. In rebuilding the west wall, however, a fine twelve-petal rose window was set in its new gable, of a type very similar to that in the rebuilt west gable of Jedburgh Abbey (*100*). There is a marked change in the masonry between the lower wall and the gable itself, which strongly suggests that the upper part of the wall, at least, was a complete rebuilding.

A stone carved with arms thought to be of Commendator James Stewart has been set in the masonry at the western end of the refectory on the side towards the cloister, which might suggest that Stewart had undertaken some rebuilding of the refectory. However, much of the reconstructed masonry in this area is clearly attributable to Lord Buchan, since his initial and the date 1788 are also to be found here, and it is perhaps also likely that it was he who set the stone with Stewart's arms into the wall (*101*).

100 Jedburgh Abbey, the west front.
Fawcett

101 Dryburgh Abbey, the arms of
Commendator James Stewart and initial
of Lord Buchan. © *Crown copyright,
reproduced courtesy of Historic Scotland*

THE WEST CONVENTUAL RANGE

We know very little about what happened on the west side of the cloister at Dryburgh. On analogy with the provisions made by the Cistercian order of monks, from whom the Premonstratensians took the idea of having lay brethren to carry out much of their manual work, it might have been expected that the accommodation and work areas for those brethren would have been in that area. That side of the cloister was, of course, generally the part of the main core of monastic buildings that was closest to the outside world, and so it was there that those functions which required contact with the world on a regular basis could be housed with least disruption to the community. The scale of accommodation that might be provided for the lay brethren at a major Cistercian abbey can be seen at Melrose, where extensive ranges that were built and progressively added to on the west side of the cloister, around an outer courtyard, have been found through excavation. However, a leading historian of British monasticism has rightly commented that very little is known about the architectural provisions that were made for the lay brethren who served Premonstratensian houses,[47] and this is certainly the case at Dryburgh, where there is no trace of buildings like those of Melrose.

If, as an alternative to following the architectural lead of the Cistercians, the Premonstratensians of Dryburgh had chosen to follow the lead of the older orders of monks and canons, the buildings on the west side of the cloister might instead have included the store-rooms of the cellarer, who was responsible for provisioning the house, or the residence of the abbot, who inevitably had to have much contact with the world outside the cloister; he would also be expected to entertain the most important visitors to the abbey without disturbing the community. There would in addition usually be at least an outer parlour in the west range, where the canons might have limited contact with layfolk.

But there is no evidence that the canons of Dryburgh followed the example of either the Cistercians or the older orders in the arrangements on the west side of the cloister; and it seems that no range running the full extent of the west side of the cloister was ever in fact built. The omission of a west range does not seem to be typical of the order as a whole, although it was certainly foreshadowed at the senior house of the order, at Prémontré itself (see *1*), as well as at Dryburgh's own mother house of Alnwick, where excavation in the 1880s revealed no trace of a west range (see *10*). Eventually, however, and probably not before the very late Middle Ages, a small building, raised above three barrel-vaulted compartments of cellars, was built at the northern end of the west wall of the cloister, adjacent to the west front of the church (see *9*). It was entered by a small doorway at the north end of the west cloister wall, and there was a single small window in the west wall of each bay; the northern compartment also had a fireplace. We have no means of knowing how many storeys were intended to be built over this basement, or what was the purpose of the building. Balancing this block, at the southern end of the west cloister wall, we have already seen that there would have been the kitchen and other offices; but otherwise it seems that the west cloister wall was always the only barrier between the cloister itself and the wider precinct of the abbey.

There is, however, the rather puzzling feature of a chamfered string course that runs the full length of the west side of the west cloister wall (see 99). It might be suggested that this is simply a feature intended to give an otherwise blank external wall an element of architectural articulation; but if that is the case, why is there not also a base course? Beyond that, it should be noted that the top surface of the moulding is flat, whereas external mouldings are more usually downward-chamfered in order to encourage rainwater to fall away. It is also significant that the wall above the string course is set back from the lower wall face. The closest parallels for this moulding at Dryburgh are with the string courses from which the barrel vaults in the sacristy, slype and chapter house spring (see 72, 76 and 77), and it may be wondered if the string course along the west cloister wall was similarly intended to mark the springing point of a barrel vault running the length of an intended, but never executed, west conventual range. It must be conceded that a continuous longitudinal barrel vault would be most unusual in a west range; two aisles of four-part vaulting would be very much more common, as in the outer parts of the east range and the original undercroft of the refectory. Nevertheless in the earlier parts of the east range the aesthetics of barrel vaulting were clearly greatly appreciated, and a west range barrel vault would probably have been no wider or more difficult to construct than that of the chapter house.

On present evidence, there can be no certainty as to whether a west range with a lower storey covered by a barrel vault was in fact ever intended, though, as has been said, the flat-topped form of the string course might be more consistent with the function of marking the springing line of a vault than as an element of mural articulation. Beyond that, despite the precedents of the absence of a west range at Prémontré and Alnwick, it is highly unusual for there to have been no west conventual range at such a major foundation. The possibility that one was intended, but was abandoned as a result of the financial difficulties in which the abbey found itself, must therefore at least be worth considering. As was mentioned in discussing the length of the nave, a geophysical survey was carried out in 2004 to determine if there was any evidence of an extended nave and west range having been set out. Following that survey it was concluded that 'it may be that the distribution of high amplitude responses are the product of a combination of wall remains, footings and foundations as well as the spread of general demolition rubble', although the evidence was insufficient to positively prove that a west range had ever been laid out. The question of whether or not a west range was intended must therefore remain open, pending further research.

THE GATEHOUSE

Careful control was exercised over those who might have access to, and the need to move within, a monastic precinct. While communities of canons had greater contact with the world than the more enclosed orders, in common with most other monasteries they generally chose to erect walls around the more vulnerable sides of their precincts. This was partly to emphasise that those precincts were enclaves of prayer and havens of contemplative peace that had to be sheltered from unnecessary intrusion; but it was also a sensible measure aimed at protecting their possessions from the predatory interests of others. Dryburgh, along with the other abbeys in southern Scotland, certainly came to have good reason to know that it was not immune from acts of war, while its great wealth might attract the covetous interests of many, particularly in the later Middle Ages, when the abbey was perhaps no longer seen to be so completely fulfilling its intended functions as fully as was once the case.

Access both into and within the precinct would be governed by a number of gatehouses; but the only one to survive is to the south-west of the refectory (*102*), where it presumably marked a line that separated inner and outer spatial envelopes. It is on the southern bank of the main water channel, on the far side

102 Dryburgh Abbey, the gatehouse. © *Crown copyright, reproduced courtesy of Historic Scotland*

of a small bridge, and is a small gabled rectangle that had arched gateways on the two main sides, and an upper floor from which it was evidently possible to reach the wall head of the bridge. Probably dating from the late fifteenth or early sixteenth century, it has the arms of two prominent local families on the skew-putts of its north-east gable, the Greenlaws and the Kers.

THE WIDER PRECINCT

The wider precinct of the abbey is likely to have been extensive, probably occupying much of the land within the loop of the Tweed on which it stood (*103*), and with a substantial precinct wall cutting off the neck of the promontory. Some idea of the range of building types that might be expected may be gained by comparison with the evidence found through excavation at Alnwick in the 1880s. There the abbey was also in a loop of the river, in that case the Alne, though the curve of the loop was rather more shallow than at Dryburgh, and the abbey was placed closer to the river. The main enclosure at Alnwick was defined to the north by a precinct wall that ran roughly parallel to the river, and the principal gate was a short distance to the north of the west front of the abbey church (see *10*). West of the church was the outer courtyard, where many of the functions that required regular contact with the outside world were concentrated. South-west of the church were what was interpreted by the excavator as guest houses and cellarer's stores, while further east were bakehouses and brewhouses. East of the church, and extending along the bank of the river were buildings likely to have been associated with the infirmary.

At Dryburgh the precinct was deeper from north to south than Alnwick, but relatively less wide from east to west. Crossing the precinct, to the south of the cloister, was an artificial channel which carried the abbey's main water supply from a cauld on the Tweed, on the west side of the promontory, and which returned to the river on the east side. As at Alnwick, there would have been a scattering of buildings within the precinct to meet the daily needs of a great religious body with major land-holdings, and which also had responsibilities for hospitality towards those who visited it. The only building to survive in recognisable form beyond the main nucleus around the cloister, however, is the small late medieval gatehouse mentioned above on the south side of a bridge across the water channel.

It cannot be ruled out that fragments of other monastic buildings within the precinct have been absorbed into more recent structures. The name of a building known as the Brewhouse, to the east of the abbey, for example, could perpetuate memories of the place where the beer for the canons was brewed, while a much modernised mill, also to the east of the abbey, may be on the site of a mill where the abbey's corn was ground. Similarly, it must also be a possibility that Dryburgh Abbey House, to the south-east, although now largely of late nineteenth-century

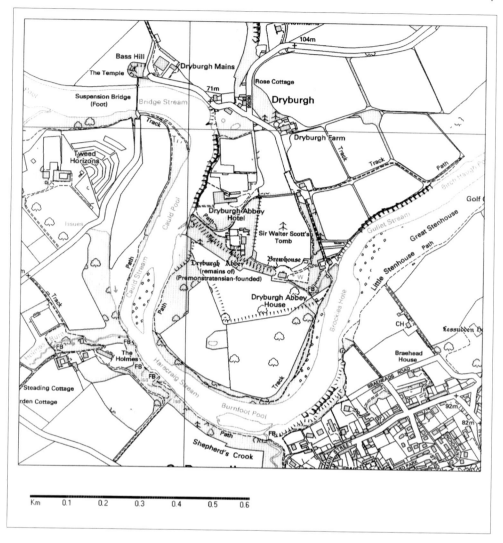

103 Dryburgh, map of the area around the abbey. © *Crown copyright, all rights reserved. Historic Scotland Licence No. 100017509, 2005*

date, is the successor of a building that once formed part of the abbey complex; this possibility might be reinforced by its location against the main water channel of the abbey, which would be a favoured location for a monastic building that required water supply and drainage.

THE ABBEY BUILDINGS AFTER THE REFORMATION

Although the Reformation Parliament of 1560 brought to an end the monastic life that had been Drybrurgh's principal reason for existence over the previous 410 years, a number of the canons are likely to have wished to continue occupying their old quarters in the abbey. It is also likely enough that at least some of the canons found it difficult to reject their old way of life immediately, and certainly in 1569 three of the canons were accused of still acting as priests. Beyond that, the abbey continued to exist as a landed corporation under the control of a branch of the Erskine family, the commendatorship having been acquired by Thomas Erskine in 1539. Eventually, in 1604, by which time all of the old community of canons had died, the estates, together with those of Cambuskenneth Abbey and Inchmahome Priory, were erected into a temporal lordship for John Erskine, second earl of Mar. He took the additional title of Lord Cardross. The adapted east range would have presumably continued to serve as an occasional residence for him and his successors for some years to come, and he is known to have carried out work on it (see above p.36). The church, however, which served no parochial functions and was no longer required for any form of worship, must have come to be regarded as little more than a quarry for building materials soon after religious life ceased, and the processes of destruction appear to have taken rapid hold.

What remained of the abbey estate was in 1682 sold to Sir Patrick Scott (see above p.38), and it was soon afterwards that the first known detailed views of the abbey were drawn, by Captain John Slezer, who published them in his *Theatrum Scotiae* of 1693 (*104* and *105*). The church appears to have been by then already very much in the state we now see, except that there may have been a little more of the window in the east wall of the south transept chapel. However, as we have seen in discussing the later alterations to the east claustral range, Slezer shows that rather more of the upper storeys of the east conventual range was surviving in the later seventeenth century than is now the case. The section of the first floor that faced on to the cloister was almost complete, and part of the second storey adjacent to the transept was also evidently standing up to the wall head (compare *69*).

The better survival of these buildings can presumably be attributed to the fact that they had continued to be occupied by the commendators for some time after the Reformation, though by the time that Slezer drew his views it was evidently only parts of the two lower storeys that remained in active use. The more distant of Slezer's two views appears to show a somewhat motley grouping of roofs, though the perspective is rather confused. One of those roofs evidently ran back from the east gable of the refectory at ninety degrees to the east range, though nothing is shown of this roof on the more detailed view. There also seems to be a roof set down within the range to its north, while the southernmost part of the east range that projected beyond the adjacent refectory

104 Dryburgh Abbey, as in 1693. Slezer *Theatrum Scotiae*

105 Dryburgh Abbey, a distant view as in 1693. Slezer *Theatrum Scotiae*

would appear to have been a separate dwelling, with its own gables and dormer windows to the upper storey. It cannot be ruled out, however, that some of the roofs visible in this view belonged to buildings behind the range. The view also suggests that the south cloister arcade still existed at that time, even if it is represented in a highly unconvincing manner, with more of the appearance of a Renaissance domestic loggia than of a monastic cloister. What appears likely, however, is that by the later seventeenth century the added upper storey of the east range had been largely abandoned, and a rather motley array of roofs had instead been contrived at a lower level within the ruined superstructure to afford protection for only parts of the building. The creases of some of those roofs are still to be seen above the sacristy and chapter house, the former being of rather low pitch, but the latter more steeply pitched (see 95).

In 1700 the estates were acquired by Thomas Haliburton, and sixty-seven years later they passed to Lieutenant-Colonel Charles Tod; but it was to be a third transfer of ownership in the course of the eighteenth century that was most significant for the abbey's fortunes. David Steuart Erskine, eleventh earl of Buchan, was a complex and fascinating character, with a deep interest in the history of the Scottish nation.[48] He also occupied an important place in the intellectual ferment associated with the Scottish Enlightenment, as is perhaps best illustrated in his being the prime mover behind the foundation of the Society of Antiquaries of Scotland in 1780. So far as Dryburgh is concerned, his interest in the nation's history was complemented by the fact that he was a descendant of the family that had once held the commendatorship of the abbey. Indeed, one of his own titles, which had passed into his branch of the Erskine family in 1698, was that of Lord Cardross, the title that had been taken by the commendator for whom the estates were erected into a temporal lordship. In view of all of this, it was perhaps only to be expected that, when the opportunity arose, he should have seized the chance to acquire the Dryburgh Abbey estates in 1786.

At first his main efforts were concentrated on making Dryburgh Abbey House, to the south-east of the abbey, a more suitable residence for himself. But by 1791 ambitious plans for the abbey itself were beginning to take shape, and in those the abbey had the merits of being not only a monument of Scotland's past, but also that increasingly valued focus in any romantically-inclined nobleman's park, an authentic and hoarily ivy-clad medieval ruin. By that stage, of course, the abbey had long suffered from being regarded as a quarry for building materials, though it is possible to detect a change in attitudes in the reasons behind that quarrying. Initially the abbey was regarded as little more than a source of cheap materials. But in the course of the eighteenth century, as awareness of the historical and aesthetic merits of medieval architecture became more wide-spread, it was increasingly the qualities of the carved stonework that were appreciated, and at least one architectural feature was removed to serve as a focus of interest elsewhere. That feature was the inner orders of the south-east

on their lands. A good example of this kind of gift can be seen in Peter de Haig's gift of property in his toun of Bemersyde. This award comprised the fifth messuage on the east side of the toun, containing the house which had been Goda his mother's, with garden attached, and it was given on the condition that the canons place a tenant and his family in it.[42] From the outset, therefore, it can be seen that Dryburgh was operating as a *rentier*, drawing a significant portion of its income from leases on properties scattered from Fife and Ayrshire to East Lothian and eastern Roxburghshire. We do not have evidence to show clearly if the canons sought to exploit any of its larger blocks of land more directly during the boom agricultural years of the later thirteenth century, but it seems clear that from the fourteenth century onwards, possibly as a consequence of the economic downturn of the early 1300s, the military instability of the region and, after about 1350, the impact of the Black Death, even the abbey's main grange properties were being let for rent.

There are two further facets to the rental income component of the abbey estate: burgh properties and mills. Examples of both types of property can be seen in the abbey's possession from its earliest development. Teind from the mills of Lauder and Saulton, for example, were in the canons' hands before 1160 and probably from 1150,[43] while Beatrice de Beauchamp was making gifts of property in Roxburgh to the abbey between 1150 and 1152.[44] Gifts of teind from mills, or indeed of outright possession of the mills, brought a major source of income into the hands of the canons. In the expanding arable-based economy of south-eastern Scotland in the later twelfth and thirteenth centuries, a property right which was founded on the render of a fixed portion of the milled grain was clearly a bountiful generator of income. Likewise, as Scotland's market economy and international trade developed, control of properties in the burghs through which all of that burgeoning trade was channelled was also likely to bring in swelling levels of rental income, especially if the properties owned by the canons were located in desirable residential and commercial streets.

Dryburgh's main burgh properties were located in two centres, Roxburgh and Lanark. As mentioned above, Beatrice de Beauchamp started the abbey's interest in the former by the gift of properties which she had specifically purchased from Roger the Janitor for the purpose.[45] About the same date, Earl Henry, David I's son, granted the canons a property outside the west gate wall of the burgh, apparently in a suburban development, while his father gave them a further property inside the same gate.[46] Further gifts came from burgess families. At the east end of the town, in the street leading to the Teviot bridge, Robert Boneire gave the canons the land which had been Edolph the Miller's.[47] The abbey had acquired further properties in the heart of the burgh by the fourteenth century, mainly in the highly desirable King's Street, and added significantly to those possessions in the 1330s through gifts from Edward III's constable of the castle, Sir William de Feltoun.[48] These acquisitions were presumably intended to permit the canons to benefit from the importance of the great international trade fair of the St James Fair held in the late summer at Roxburgh, where they could easily dispose of their produce to the many merchants who were drawn there by the wool produced by the Border abbeys. Unfortunately for the canons, their investment in Roxburgh was not to prove beneficial in the long term as the burgh went into sharp decline from the later fourteenth century and eventually disappeared entirely in the first half of the fifteenth century, just when the abbey most needed a cash injection to pay for reconstruction work after its burning by Richard II.

The abbey's other significant concentration of burgh properties was in Lanark. In the twelfth and thirteenth centuries, Lanark was one of the main burghs of southern Scotland and had been in the 'big four' of the trading centres of David I's kingdom. Dryburgh's connection with the town originated with David's grant to the canons of the parish church of St Kentigern of the burgh (see below p.168), but other gifts followed of burgages in Lanark granted by ordinary townsmen such as Humphrey the Horn-worker.[49] The canons maintained their interests in the burgh down to the Reformation, administering the collection of their rents through their grange of Inglisberry.

Unlike Melrose, the canons of Dryburgh do not appear to have been involved directly in international trade and, whilst they acquired property at nearby Roxburgh which seems to have been aimed at benefiting from the commercial activity of that burgh they did not actively develop a similar presence in Scotland's main trading outlet, Berwick-upon-Tweed. Berwick had a major urban presence by the Scottish monasteries, several of whom sought to establish their own business centre in the port as well as to develop a portfolio of rental properties in this thriving commercial community. Melrose in particular controlled a major block of burgages and built a substantial house in the town from which the abbot's representatives could oversee their trading interests.[50] Dryburgh's presence was on an altogether smaller scale and seems to have been purely intended as a source of rental income, as a gift in 1275 of a burgage in the Ravensdean area of Berwick by John Dunbar, burgess of the town, makes explicit.[51] It seems that their other burgh properties, located in Haddington and Dunbar in East Lothian, and Anstruther and Crail in Fife, were regarded in a similar way.

Mills and mill teinds provided a significant revenue stream throughout the abbey's existence. The original award of the teinds from Lauder and Saulton was supplemented by about 1153 by Beatrice de Beauchamp's gift of the teind of the mill of Nenthorn.[52] Sometime after 1162, Richard de Morville's sister, Ada, granted the canons the teind of the mill of Newton, while in the late 1100s Thomas of Thirlstane gave then the teind of his mill of Thirlstane,[53] which gave them a convenient group of mills from which they drew income in Tweeddale and Lauderdale, north and east of the abbey. Thomas's descendant, William Maitland, subsequently freed the canons from payment of multure and other services at Thirlstane mill.[54] These gifts, however, were simply of revenue from the mills rather than physical possession of the mills themselves. Where the canons were developing a significant property interest, as for example in Saulton and Eldbottle in East Lothian, actual possession of a mill themselves would have been a considerable economic benefit, as they would no longer have been liable for payment of multures on the grain ground in the local lords' mills. In the early 1220s they received the right to have their own mill (with an associated brewhouse) at Easter Fenton near Dirleton,[55] which would thereafter have served their large concentration of arable lands in that vicinity.

One interesting addition to the abbey's portfolio of mills came in the early fourteenth century. In 1293, Sir William de Abernethy granted the canons two merks annually from the multures of his mill of Oxton in Lauderdale to pay for lights at the image of the Blessed Virgin in the abbey church.[56] The abbey appears to have received the rights to the teind of Oxton before 1238, when the bishop of St Andrews confirmed their possession, but this was to be expanded into full possession the following century.[57] Probably in the 1330s, Sir William's son and successor, also Sir William de Abernethy, granted Dryburgh his mill at Oxton, with the right to collect multure and other fruits. The grant, however, was conditional, with William requiring that the canons accept him, his wife and heirs into their fraternity.[58] This was an agreement which obligated the canons to provide in perpetuity for the inclusion of the Abernethys in the masses and prayers of the community with full benefits, as though they were members of the convent. In an age preoccupied increasingly with spiritual welfare, this was a common method of providing for the future salvation of the souls of the donor and their designated kinsmen.

Again, where the canons possessed the mill or rights to collect multures or teind, they would not be operating it themselves. Only at Dryburgh itself, and possibly at Easter Fenton, is it likely that the canons, or rather their servitors, operated the mill directly. At Oxton, it is more probable that the mill was leased to a miller, who would have given the canons an agreed share of the profits from the milling operations and pocketed the rest. The mill teinds and teinds of multures which the canons held would probably also have been farmed out to collectors, who would have paid the abbey a cash equivalent rather than delivered to them the render in kind.

Overall, we can see that from the twelfth century that whilst the canons were lords of land on a not entirely insignificant scale their chief source of income was from rents. This had the advantage of giving them a fairly secure level of cash income, which should have permitted them to plan for future developments. Before 1200, most of their outlying properties were paying cash rents and remitting the funds to the abbey. Their main landed properties seem to have been run primarily as granges, either for supplying the monastic household itself (as was the case with Kedslie, Dryburgh itself and the lands around Mertoun and Brotherstone/Smailholm) or as market producers which disposed of their grain and wool yields at more local markets (probably Edinburgh or Haddington for

Saltoun and Eldbottle and Lanark for Inglisberry). It is quite a radically different picture from that which we have for Melrose Abbey and the Cistercian order in general, and highlights the diversity of the nature of ecclesiastical estate management, and indeed of the ecclesiastical estates, in medieval Scotland.

CHURCHES

Unlike the various orders of monks, whose rules prohibited them from accepting control of the patronage of parish churches, serving them with one of their number, or drawing parish revenues for the support of their communities, canons-regular had no qualms about any of these matters (*114*). Indeed, the apostolic tradition of the canons was well-suited to their serving the wider Christian community as preachers and priests, and from the first control of parish churches and parish revenues constituted an important element in the portfolios of land, revenues and rights accumulated by Premonstratensian houses for their support.

Control of churches contributed to the revenues of the abbey from the time of its foundation and at various times down to the Reformation it possessed nineteen in Scotland (although never all simultaneously) and two others in England.[59] Included in the original endowment were the churches and associated church-lands of Channelkirk in Lauderale, Mertoun in Tweeddale (just 2km north-east of Dryburgh), and Asby in Westmorland.[60] The church of St Cuthbert of Channelkirk, which lies at the head of Lauderdale, offers a good illustration of the problems and potentials which possession of parish churches presented. St Cuthbert's was described in the thirteenth century as the original 'mother-church' of the valley,[61] and its dedication to the greatest of the Northumbrian saints suggests that its origins lay possibly as early as the eighth or ninth centuries. Its parish was extensive, apparently originally covering the whole of the valley from its head to between Lauder and Earlston, and it seems likely that the teinds due to it and other income from lands, rents and rights bestowed on it would have constituted a potentially substantial source of income. It may have been Hugh's intention that the full revenues of Channelkirk and the other churches would pass directly to Dryburgh, but what he actually granted was probably only the rights of patronage which he held as lord of Lauderdale.

Control of the patronage alone was unsatisfactory for most monasteries. They were seeking regular sources of income and where they only possessed patronage rights that income would be intermittent, for they were simply being given the right to appoint the parish priest. For the Premonstratensians that was less of a problem than for the orders of monks, for canons were also priests and were permitted by their rule to undertake pastoral duties in parish churches and as preachers. Dryburgh could – and did – install its own canons as parish clergy in churches given to it, but there remained the added problem of the revenues of the

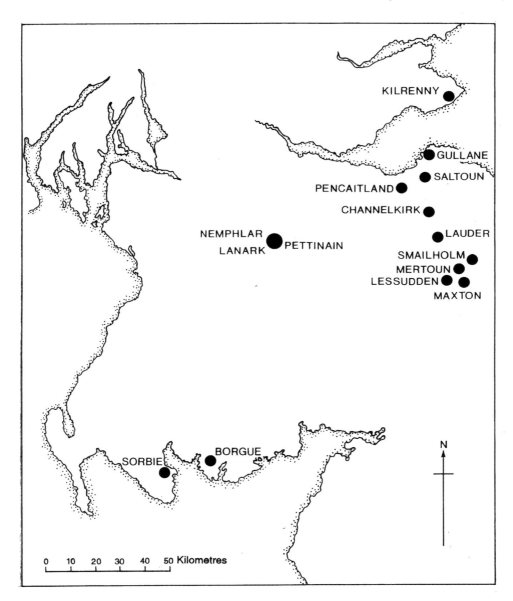

114 Distribution map of churches held by Dryburgh Abbey in Scotland before 1350. *Sylvia Stevenson/Historic Scotland*

parish, which were intended for the support of its priest. Like other regular clergy, the Premonstratensians took vows of personal poverty, which meant that they themselves could not benefit directly from the income provided by the parish. That income would instead have to be made over to their monastery, a process known as appropriation. No formal mechanism, however, existed to permit that, and bishops were reluctant to see revenues diverted away from the localities to possibly distant monasteries, with no adequate provision being set in place to ensure that there was a good quality of spiritual service offered to parishioners or that the church building was maintained in good order. By the later twelfth century, there was a recognised problem of absentee clergy who were canons in monasteries, who were simply installing poorly-paid and ill-trained curates to undertake their duties. Eventually, the papacy intervened to provide a solution and at the Fourth Lateran Council of 1215 Pope Innocent III decreed that '…as he who lives of the altar serves of the altar … a sufficient portion be assigned for the priest'.[62] The result of this was the institution of formal arrangements to provide a standard of service at parish level that would satisfy the bishop. In the thirteenth century, the formula adopted was for a division of the income into two components, parsonage teinds and vicarage teinds, with the former being appropriated to the controlling monastery and the latter being assigned for the support of the vicar who would undertake the absentee parson or rector's duties. Such arrangements had still to satisfy the bishop, who would confirm them with a charter containing the phrase *in proprios usus*, a formula which permitted the appropriator to divert his share of the revenues to the uses of the monastery. Between about 1220 and 1260, there was a flood of such settlements confirmed by charter around Scotland as bishops and appropriators attempted to regularise the chaotic arrangements already in place.

At Channelkirk, there is no formal charter granting the canons the parsonage teinds, but in about 1220, when William Malveisin, bishop of St Andrews, confirmed the canons' possession of the church it is implicit that it was already held *in proprios usus*.[63] The parish revenues must have contributed very significantly to the abbey's income, for when in March 1268 Bishop Gamelin set in place a settlement to provide adequate payment for vicars of Dryburgh's appropriated churches in St Andrews diocese, the vicar of Channelkirk received the largest stipend (£10), reflecting the wealth of this extensive parish.[64] This settlement held for the remainder of the Middle Ages, with no attempt being made by the canons to get their hands on the vicarage revenues as well as the parsonage teinds, something common in the vast majority of Scottish parishes.

The 1268 settlement also marked the end of a long-running dispute over the status of the church of Lauder. This church had probably originated as a chapel serving the household of the de Morvilles there and had originally been dependent on the parish church of Channelkirk. Such private chapels within larger parishes were not uncommon, two others being established at Glengelt and Carfrae in Channelkirk by their de Mundeville and Sinclair lords,[65] but their relationship with the mother church of the parish was usually carefully regulated to ensure that income intended for the parish priest was not diverted away from him. Such careful regulation can be seen most clearly in Dryburgh's case in respect of its church of Gullane in East Lothian, where the de Vaux lords of Dirleton, who founded chapels of St Andrew and All Saints at their caput in the early thirteenth century, were required to confirm their chaplains' 'fealty' to the rector of Gullane and arrange for payments of cash, wax and incense which symbolised their subordination to the priest of the mother-church.[66] Lauder chapel, however, may have been established in the 1130s or 1140s when Hugh de Morville developed his lordship centre at Lauder, before procedures for formalising the creation of new parishes or for regulating relationships between parish churches and dependent chapels had been instituted. Before the end of the twelfth century it appears to have somehow managed to acquire parish status and secured assignment to it of teinds from the surrounding territory. One of the de Morville lords, probably William, had evidently granted certain of those teinds to Kilwinning Abbey, but Dryburgh also believed that it possessed rights to them as possessor of Channelkirk. Following a judgement in 1221 at Irvine, in 1228 Dryburgh and Kilwinning abbeys had reached agreements, confirmed by papal bulls, over their conflicting rights from the 'parish' and over the patronage of the 'church' of Lauder.[67] Despite that settlement, by 1246 the canons were having to pursue a court action against Master Eymeric, rector of Lauder, over payment of teinds, the litigation dragging on until 1252 when papal judges–delegate found in favour of the abbey.[68] The deciding factor in favour of the canons had been their claim that Lauder was a dependency of Channelkirk and did not have any status as an independent parish. In their definitive sentence against Eymeric, his charge was referred to only as a chapel, not a church. The uncertainty, however, was resolved only in June 1268 when Dervorgilla of Galloway and her husband, John Balliol, resigned the patronage to the canons, who were obliged thereafter to provide six chaplains to say masses in it for their souls and for all their ancestors and successors.[69]

Conflict over control of teinds arose in the early thirteenth century in respect of most of the parish churches that Dryburgh possessed. The number of disputes and court actions in the earlier 1220s that revolved around collection and payment of teind suggests that most were triggered by Pope Innocent III's 1215 decree, which forced monastic appropriators to regularise the often shambolic arrangements and over-lapping (and often contradictory) grants by which they had obtained control of the revenues. As with Lauder, different monastic communities held what they believed to be rights to the same parish revenues. In Gullane parish, Dryburgh's interests collided with those of the Cistercian nunnery of Southberwick, or Berwick-on-Tweed. In April 1221, William de Vaux of Dirleton granted the canons serving in the church of St Nicholas on the island of Edlbottle, the patronage of the church of Gullane and all his other rights in that church. His charter, however, excluded certain unspecified rights in the church which he had already made over to the nuns of Southberwick.[70] Dryburgh's case was strengthened by confirmations of the grant at the same time by William's son, John, who reserved also the interest in the parish of his younger brother, William, the then rector of Gullane. The nuns, however, had challenged Dryburgh's possession and in a settlement imposed by Master James, the papal legate to Scotland received confirmation of certain elements of teind income, for example from the lands of Kingston, and relating to the chapels of Eldbottle and Dirleton, but renounced all claims which they had on the parish church itself.[71] The parish was shortly thereafter confirmed *in proprios usus* to Dryburgh, with reservation of the agreed teinds to the nuns,[72] an arrangement which held until 1391, when the nunnery's Scottish possessions were all made over to the canons (see above pp.27-28).

Kilrenny in Fife brought Dryburgh into another dispute of a different sort over teind income. The church was granted to the canons in about 1160 by Countess Ada, mother of Kings Malcolm IV and William the Lion, and confirmed in their possession in a papal bull of Pope Alexander III the following year.[73] It seems only to have been through a fresh grant of the church by William, earl of Buchan, in about 1220 that the canons secured possession, reinforced by a series of confirmations by Master James, the papal legate, and Bishop William Malveisin of St Andrews, while in 1228 Pope Gregory IV confirmed the appropriation.[74] In 1268, as part of Bishop Gamelin's vicarage settlement for all of the churches at that date appropriated to Dryburgh in his see, it was confirmed *in proprios usus* to the canons and a stipend of 10 merks assigned to the vicar.[75] Despite the difficulties in actually securing possession in the twelfth century, the situation appeared uncontroversial, but the development of commercial fishing in the Firth of Forth introduced a new and potentially very lucrative dimension to the teind income which both Dryburgh and other local parties were keen to secure for themselves.

Kilrenny's fishing teinds had already emerged as a source of dispute with the priory at St Andrews before 1222. A composition was settled between the monasteries which agreed that the fishermen of the parish of Kilrenny who moored and unloaded in the port of St Andrews would pay no teind to St Andrews priory, but would render instead to their mother church of Kilrenny and vice versa for the fishermen of St Andrews in the parish of Kilrenny.[76] Three years later, however, a similar dispute with the Cluniac priory on the Isle of May could not be settled so amicably and the case was eventually brought before papal judges-delegate. The heart of the dispute lay in a question of where the fishing-boats operating out of the stream-mouth haven of Anstruther were moored and where the fishermen were resident. The settlement at the stream mouth lay on either side of the Dreel Burn, which still divides the modern community into the distinct villages of Anstruther Easter and Anstruther Wester. While Anstruther Easter lay in the parish of Kilrenny, Anstruther Wester lay in Anstruther parish, which was possessed by the monks of May.[77] The boundary between the two parishes was considered, by Dryburgh at least, to run down the middle channel of the Dreel Burn, and that boats which moored to the east of that line and whose crews lived in Kilrenny parish should pay teind to that church. The monks of May, however, whose greater proximity to Anstruther enabled them to interfere to their own benefit, were diverting all teind from Anstruther Easter fishermen to their own church in Anstruther Wester. Dryburgh was prepared to compromise and was seeking only half of the teind of the fishermen, and it was on that basis that the judges-delegate decided. From December 1225, the monks of May were obliged to pay 1 merk of silver annually to the church of Kilrenny in lieu of teind.[78] The sums involved in such disputes were hardly huge, but given the parlous state of Dryburgh's finances at this time every penny counted.

The issue of distance from Dryburgh which may have been a factor in its problems at Kilrenny was an even greater element of the difficulties which the abbey encountered over its interest in the remotest of its churches, Bozeat in Northamptonshire.[79] Bozeat was part of the property which Beatrice de Beauchamp brought into the de Morville family at the time of her marriage to Hugh the Constable. Soon after the foundation of Dryburgh, she granted the church 'from her free dower, for the love of God and the remission of her sins', to the canons.[80] The gift appeared straightforward enough, and although the great distance which lay between Dryburgh and Bozeat may have made the collection of income from the church difficult, the canons certainly intended to exercise their rights to it. Needless to say, matters were far more complicated, for Bozeat and the de Morville estates lay within the earldom of Huntingdon-Northampton, which was contested between the Scots and Earl Simon II de St Liz. Earl Simon had given Bozeat to one of his own supporters, who had subsequently granted the church to the Augustinian canons of St James's abbey Northampton. While Earl Simon held the earldom, there was little prospect of Dryburgh being able to make good its claim.

Simon de St Liz died in 1153, but it was not until 1157 that the earldom of Huntingdon was restored to the Scottish crown by the new English king, Henry II.[81] As a consequence of that restoration, the de Morvilles regained possession of their estates in Northamptonshire and looked to put their gift of Bozeat into effect. A compromise deal with St James's was reached, whereby it was agreed that Dryburgh would possess the church but that St James's would hold it in return for payment of an annual pension to the canons, which Dryburgh would send a messenger to collect.[82] What had seemed like a satisfactory arrangement which had secured the canons at least some income swiftly became a source of dissatisfaction, with them complaining of the inconvenience of collecting payment.[83] With finances always tight at Dryburgh, however, they were not simply prepared to give up on the deal and looked for alternative mechanisms to manage the collection of the pension. Their first attempt was to employ the Premonstratensians of Sulby as their agent, but a yet more efficient means of securing their income soon presented itself in an exchange deal with another Northamptonshire monastery.

The opportunity to come to such an arrangement originated in a tragic accident in the early 1170s, when Richard de Morville's younger brother, Malcolm, had been killed in a hunting accident by Adulf de St Martin, brother of Alexander de St Martin, an important East Lothian landholder. In reconciliation for Malcolm's death, Alexander granted Dryburgh his lands of Bangly, north of Haddington, and also arranged that the abbey should pay an annual rent of 10s or half a carucate of land in Bangly to the abbey of St Mary Delapré at Leicester, where Malcolm de Morville had been buried.[84] Dryburgh, however, had failed to make the agreed payments and St Mary Delapré's complaint was brought before a general chapter of the Premonstratensians at Newsham in February 1193. There, Leicester formally surrendered its claims on Bangly in return for an annual payment of 5s to be paid to it from the Bozeat pension, which St James's was instructed to pay to them directly.[85] This was a very satisfactory deal for the canons, for not only had they removed a burden on a property in East Lothian where they were actively developing a significant landed interest (see above pp.153-154), and had halved the level of payments to be made, but they had offset the payments against a pension which they already faced difficulties in collecting. All that remained for them to do was find a way of collecting the balance of the money from Bozeat.

This they succeeded in doing in the 1240s, in the middle of the abbey's gravest financial crisis, when they arranged another exchange arrangement with another Northampton monastery, the Cluniac priory of St Andrew. In the early 1200s the priory had received a number of small grants of rental income or pensions from land in Lauderdale and Tweeddale from Helen de Morville and her sons, Alan, lord of Galloway, and Thomas, earl of Atholl, in recognition of the burial there of her husband and their father, Roland, lord of Galloway. He had died at Northampton in November 1200 whilst pursuing a court case involving some of Helen's inherited estates there.[86] St Andrew's must have experienced the same problems of collection as faced Dryburgh at Bozeat and presumably had placed the lands in the hands of administrators. In 1243, the obvious solution was for St Andrew's to give Dryburgh its Lauderdale property at Newbigging, while Dryburgh made over its pension from Bozeat to the priory, with the stipulation that 5s were to be paid to St Mary's Delapré and a small balance of 20d being left for the Dryburgh canons.[87] Dryburgh's perseverance in refusing simply to abandon its interest in its distant Northamptonshire church had finally paid off and its elusive pension had been converted into a useful portion of property close to its main concentration of monastic lands.

Similar problems of distance bedevilled Dryburgh's role as a would-be appropriator in south-west Scotland. Sometime between about 1162 and 1173, the canons received the gift of the church of Borgue in Galloway, probably from Hugh de Morville the younger.[88] It had for long been assumed that this grant had been made by Hugh's father around the time that he founded Dryburgh, but a strong case has been made for it being a gift from his elder son, who had received the lordship of north Westmorland from Henry II.[89] The canons do not seem to have been able to make good their possession, probably because of the civil conflict that convulsed Galloway after 1174 and the hostile regime which held power there down to 1185. The inheritance of the de Morville estates by the lords of Galloway at the end of the twelfth century brought the church more firmly into Dryburgh's hands, for in the 1230s one of Alan of Galloway's knights, Sir Ralph de Campania, to whom he had given the lordship of Borgue, re-granted the patronage to the canons.[90] Before about 1250, control of the patronage was converted by the Bishop of Whithorn into a grant *in proprios usus*, and a vicarage settlement set in place which provided a stipend of 6 merks and a glebe of six acres of arable and one of meadow.[91] Unfortunately, due to the loss of the later sections of Dryburgh's fifteenth-century cartulary, Borgue drops from view, but when it re-emerges in the surviving records in 1427, control of it lay in the hands of the Premonstratensian priory at Whithorn.[92] How and when had that transfer occurred?

The answer may lie in the experience of Dryburgh's other Galloway church, Sorbie. The parishes of Greater and Lesser Sorbie in Wigtownshire had been gifted to the abbey by the de Vieuxpont lords of Sorbie, who were kinsmen of the de Morvilles and tenants of the lords of Galloway. The patronage of Greater Sorbie had been given to the canons by Ivo de Vieuxpont, probably in the 1190s, and the church had been confirmed to them *in proprios usus* by the bishop of Whithorn shortly after 1200.[93] Lesser Sorbie was given to Dryburgh by Robert de Vieuxpont, and confirmed to the canons *in proprios usus* before 1235.[94] These were small parishes but were located in the heart of what was the agricultural heartland of western Galloway and were probably comparatively well endowed[95] and rich in teind income. It is difficult to avoid cynicism when it is recorded that Dryburgh, in the midst of its financial woes of the 1230s and 1240s, had appealed to the bishop of Whithorn for the amalgamation of the two parishes into one because 'it is indecent that the house of the Lord be demeaned by such poverty, and that those ministering in it should not be able to repair it' and that the united parishes could sustain one vicar and not the two incumbents then in place.[96] The argument was that the income of two separate parishes could not support a vicar in both and cover the maintenance costs of the two parish churches. The bishop accepted their plea and Dryburgh was permitted to divert a greater proportion of the revenues from the now united parish to their own uses, installing a single vicar on a stipend that was presumably set at a level below what had been paid to the two previous incumbents.

Highly beneficial to Dryburgh though this arrangement was, it still left the basic problem of collection of the income due from a parish that was remote from the abbey. Clearly, the canons encountered grave difficulties in securing their money and in 1282 they struck a deal with the Premonstratensian canons of Whithorn, whereby Whithorn took over Dryburgh's rights in the parish in return for an annual payment of 20 merks, plus a penalty of an extra half merk to be paid for every fifteen days that the annual sum was in arrears. The payment, interestingly, was to be made to the 'master of the works of the church of Dryburgh', suggesting that perhaps the building operations commenced in the late twelfth century were still incomplete at the end of the followingcentury.[97]

Although there is no surviving documentary evidence to establish this suggestion, it seems likely that the transfer of possession of Borgue to Whithorn occurred at the same time as the transfer of Sorbie. Just as in the case of Bozeat, the canons were seeking a mechanism that would give a secure income in return for one that was difficult, and possibly expensive, to collect. The Whithorn payment was a substantial sum and, when added to any payment for Borgue, represented a significant and secure injection of funds into the abbey's treasury. The mechanisms for payment, moreover, clearly worked, and the payments for the churches of Galloway were still being received down to the Reformation and beyond.[98]

Of the nineteen or so churches which Dryburgh at one time or other possessed, the majority came into the abbey's possession before the middle of the thirteenth century. Clearly, for would-be lay patrons, the gift of the patronage of the parish churches on their estates was a comparatively painless way of signalling their support for the abbey. At a time when the Church was actively promoting the principle that it was sinful for laymen to control what were, in effect, spiritual interests, many secular lords killed two birds with one stone by making a formal gift of their proprietory rights in parish churches and chapels and thereby safeguarding their mortal souls which had been imperilled by their possession of the patronage. It also avoided the drain on real property which many lesser lords who wished to demonstrate their support for religion and concern for their own spiritual welfare could ill afford. Although they lost the potentially lucrative or convenient gift of the presentation of the parish priest, they had not otherwise eroded deeply into their own landed reserves.

At Dryburgh, gifts of patronage were evidently a way of demonstrating support comparatively cheaply. King David I, for example, who otherwise made only some minor grants of property and rental income, used gifts of the advowsons of various churches on his estates to signal his support for his constable's efforts. Thus, in the first two years of the abbey's existence, he gave them the patronage of the churches and chapels of Lanark and Pettinain, to which his grandson, William the Lion, later added Nemphar and Cartland.[99] The canons secured the grant of Lanark and its satellite chapels *in proprios usus* before the close of the twelfth century, which enabled them to divert the substantial teind income of this flourishing burgh church and its hinterland to the needs of the abbey.[100] These kinds of grants also brought subsequent benefits to the canons as local lords, burgesses and even wealthy peasants either gave additional gifts directly to the canons, or made gifts to the parish church which benefited the canons indirectly. At Lanark and Pettinain, for example, the canons acquired both rural properties and also rental income from properties in the royal burgh.[101] As the number of confirmations of Dryburgh's possession of its churches *in proprios usus* grew through the late twelfth and thirteenth centuries, the economic value of these generously endowed parish churches for the abbey also grew significantly.

Fresh gifts of churches continued to flow into Dryburgh's possession as late as the fourteenth century. As in the earlier period, these grants were made by lords who wished to demonstrate commitment to a monastery which had suffered considerably in the warfare of previous generations, but who were also displaying awareness of the much greater emphasis being placed by the Church on what were known as *pro anima* grants (gifts for the benefit of the souls of named beneficiaries) while also seeking to minimise the capital expense. This can be seen, for example, in the Maxwells' grant to the abbey of the church of Pencaitland, or the Stewarts' grant of Maxton (just downstream from the abbey on the south side of the river).[102] For a monastery that needed a secure cash flow as it attempted to repair the fire-damage of 1322 and 1385, the dependable stream of revenue afforded by control of parishes in this way was very welcome.

One concomitant of the abbey's possession of rights in parish churches was the steady increase of the provision of one of the canons to hold the office of parson in those churches. Where vicars were provided to serve the cure, there was no requirement for the canons to reside at or serve in person in the church of which they were nominally the priest. There was, however, no stricture under the Premonstratensian rule which would have prevented a canon from serving a parish church and it is evident that at an early date members of the community were based at churches remote from the abbey. For example, by the early 1200s it appears that more than one canon was resident at the chapel of St Nicholas on the island of Fidra,[103] which seems to have acted in some way as the supervisory base for Dryburgh's East Lothian interests before the development of its Eldbottle and Saltoun estates. It is likely that the churches located closer to the abbey also were served more regularly by the canons who were nominated to the charge but by the sixteenth century there is no clear evidence that individual canons were serving any of the local parishes and the parsonage teinds and other appropriated were simply being pooled communally and divided into portions for all of the community to enjoy. By that period, the income from the parishes was effectively treated as a component of the abbey's secular estate rather than a spiritual item, and when the monastery was converted into a secular lordship the canons' rights of patronage and control of teind revenues were simply subsumed into the Erskines' private portfolio.

THE END OF THE MONASTIC ESTATE

After the handful of royal grants made in the twelfth century, further signs of royal favour came late to Dryburgh and stemmed from the prominence of its commendator in national political life. In 1527, the Douglas regime which controlled the person of the young King James V issued charters in favour of the commendator, erecting the settlement which had developed outside the gate of the abbey precinct into a burgh of barony.[104] This was a significant economic privilege for the canons, for the inhabitants – or *indwellers* – of the toun had previously been required to travel to Kelso or Duns to dispose of their produce at market. The charter now gave them the status of burgesses and empowered them to buy and sell goods in their own market – which was to be held weekly on Tuesdays and with an annual fair on the vigil of the Feast of St Thomas the Martyr – to elect baillies to oversee the good running of their community, to collect tolls on goods brought in to their market, and to have the individual house plots in the little 'burgh' measured and set out regularly in 'burghal perches'.

The burgh disappears from historical record almost as soon as it was founded, probably as a consequence of the economic decline of the abbey following its burning in the 1540s, and the community that clustered near the abbeys gates to the north of the precinct was referred to simply as 'the toun' or Dryburgh throughout the later sixteenth and seventeenth centuries. Despite its market cross, weekly market and annual fairs, the 'burgh' had never been likely to have developed into anything more than a focus for very local trade, particularly given the rival burgh developments at Kelso and Melrose, and the much older centre at Lauder.

What the short-lived burgh of Dryburgh does is underscore the misleadingly secluded aspect which the abbey ruins have in their current state. Later sixteenth-century documents paint an altogether different picture of the immediate environs of the abbey precinct and contain a detailed record of the gradual breakdown of the former religious exclusivity of that area as blocks of its estates were disposed of to various lay tenants. The most detailed record is a Great Seal confirmation of April 1581 of a charter of David Erskine, dated 24 February 1581.[105] It is a record of the granting at feuferme to Ninian Bruce, of a substantial amount of the inner core of the monastic complex. The main block comprised 38 acres of land in the toun of Dryburgh, occupied by six named tenants with portions ranging from 16 acres down to half an acre. A second block, of 21 acres, was occupied or worked by fourteen tenants. The grant included their houses, gardens and common pasture rights in the woods of Dryburgh and at Howdenhaugh. This land lay to the north of the precinct of the abbey. In addition, Bruce was granted a tenanted house in 'lie Byre-grene', a second tenanted house on the east side of the toun, and the house beside the old burgh market cross. This cluster may have lain outside the main gate into the precinct on the north, roughly where the modern village lies. Interestingly, it gives as a locational marker for the second of these houses the fulling mill, which is first mentioned in the twelfth century. The details of property then move inside the precinct wall, where Ninian was given five of the gardens belonging to the abbey. The first of these is described as lying on the south side of 'lie Lady-yett', a gateway that may have lain towards the west end of the boundary across the neck of the peninsula occupied by the abbey. The second lay beside 'lie Mantill-wall' (enclosing wall) of what is called a 'new garden' on the west of the precinct, and bounded by what were described as the 'ruinous walls' of the abbey's bakehouse and brewhouse, a tenanted house, and the mill-dam lade belonging to the toun-mill. This garden was occupied by one of the three remaining canons, Robert Mylne. A third garden, occupied by the canon James Jamesoun, lay to the south of the garden occupied by the third of the canons, Kentigern Wilson, and bounded also by the mill-lade.[106] The fourth garden, which is not specifically located, was named the Cunein-yard, while the fifth is not identified at all. In addition to these, he was given the three vaults on the west side of the cloister wall, which can still be seen. A second feu charter of May 1581 granted away further tenanted properties in and around the precinct.[107] This included a block of 'waste' on the west side of the 'Mantilwall' or precinct wall, between a garden held by one of the tenants of the toun on the south and a larger tenanted ground to the north. Additionally, it granted two further named gardens in the precinct (those known as 'Vulwartyard' and 'Jakkiswall', and two 'granary gardens', which presumably lay beside the abbey barns.

The picture which this presents to us is of a crowded landscape both within and around the precinct. Tenanted properties were built or laid out right up to the outer face of the enclosing wall, while inside the enclosure most of the space had been divided into a series of yards and gardens even before the Reformation. From these two charters, we can identify at least ten gardens inside the precinct, all apparently to the west side of the main complex of the church and cloister, and there were probably others. What is most interesting, however, is that these gardens seem originally to have been the private portions of the canons, providing us with evidence that Dryburgh experienced the common late medieval trend of individual members of the community receiving their own portions of the abbey property to manage and dispose of as they saw fit. The canons evidently continued to live in the cloister, no separate houses or manses for them being mentioned within the precinct, but presumably as at Melrose they had divided up the dormitory and infirmary to provide themselves with private rooms rather than common sleeping and working quarters. It is probably safe to assume that before the Reformation these gardens remained in the hands of individual canons but after 1560, as the community slowly died off, David Erskine began to rent them out to lay tenants, gradually nibbling away at the once exclusive character of the precinct.

Long before the precinct was invaded, the abbey's landed properties had begun to be disposed of in a haphazard manner. From the mid 1530s, James Stewart presided over a regime which saw the progressive erosion of the abbey estate through the grant of tacks and feuferme charters to tenants, vassals and political associates. While presented as heritable tenancies, the setting of the abbey land to these laymen effectively amounted to permanent alienation of the property, with the canons remaining nominal superiors in return for a fairly small annual money rent. The process had begun in the later fifteenth century, possibly as a response to the monastery's continuing need for ready cash to pay for the rebuilding work necessary after the 1443 fire. The reconstruction after that fire was still causing financial headaches in 1461 when the canons appealed to the pope for a bull of protection (see above p.29) and it may be purely coincidental that the earliest surviving tack of abbey lands dates from only four years later. On 16 November 1465, Abbot Walter issued a tack to a local laird, William

Haliburton of Mertoun, and his wife, Janet, of the life-rent of the Plewland of Butchercots in Smailholm parish, for an annual payment of forty shillings 'of gud and usuale money of Scotland'.[108] In return, the Haliburtons probably received a piece of land which the abbey had held since the 1150s, given to it by David Olifard soon after its foundation and confirmed in its possession in the 1320s by Andrew Moray following the burning of Dryburgh in 1322.[109] It amounted to around 120 acres of arable land plus common pasture for 300 sheep. All told, from the Haliburtons' perspective, this was a good deal.

Under James Stewart the pace and scale of erosion of the abbey's property increased dramatically. In May 1536, he issued a charter to Master Andrew Hume, brother of David Hume of Wedderburn, and to Andrew's bastard son William, in return for a cash payment of 280 merks made by Andrew for the maintenance of the monastery and as contribution towards the king's general taxation. For this service, Andrew received all of the kirklands of Lauder, comprising Spittal, Snawdon, Newbigging and properties in Lauder itself, valued at 25 merks, which had previously been granted to him by the canons in lieu of a pension, and which were united into a single lordship of Spittal, for an annual rent of 32 merks, 25 capons and 25 hens.[110] This was a significant alienation, removing from the abbey's future control a large block of property in central Lauderdale, much of it consisting of good-quality arable land and pasture. At a time when property values were increasing and produce prices on the market rising, it made little sense for the canons to be disposing of land for so little return on it. The alienation of the Lauder kirklands, however, marked only the start of a general trend.

It was another Haliburton, Walter, and his wife Agnes Stewart, who benefited from the next feuferme grant made by James Stewart. The original award does not survive, but a notarial instrument of 12 June 1537, drawn up following a meeting of the convent gathered in the chapterhouse, set out the terms of their joint infeftment in the abbey's lands of Nether Shielfield, setting the lands for an annual rent of 6s 8d.[111] This transaction was just the first in a flood of grants which saw the effective alienation of significant portions of the monastic estate around Dryburgh itself, such as the large block of arable land in Mertoun which was set for nineteen years to the sitting tenant, Thomas Myll, for an annual rent of two merks.[112] It was possibly the same Walter Haliburton, described as 'of Mertoun', a descendant of William Haliburton of the 1465 tack, who received a feuferme grant of the same lands of Butchercotes in Smailholm parish in September 1538. Rehearsing the familiar jingle that the grant was being made in recognition of the cash gifts he had made towards the 'sustenance and repair of the monastery' – possibly relating to damage inflicted by the English in the desultory raiding that occurred in the aftermath of Flodden – and towards payment of the general tax which the king was levying on the Church with papal authorisation for the endowment of the College of Justice, Butchercotes was set heritably to Walter, to pass to his bastard son and apparent heir, Andrew, for 46s 8d, an increase of one sixth on the rent that the Haliburtons had been paying for this same land since 1465.[113] The benefit to the monastery was fairly minimal and the canons had lost the ability to let the land to the highest bidder.

A feuferme charter of 1 November 1537 narrates the supposed reasons behind this policy of alienation, stating that it arose from recent parliamentary legislation aimed at improving the 'common weal' of the kingdom, which called for the granting 'in feu ferme and heretage' of lands belonging to 'the king and utheris prelattis, temporall Lordes, Erles, Barrones and the lands possest be other men'. The land was to be granted out without diminution of rental income due from them to the superior lord, but in such a way as to give the tenants an interest in them that would encourage them to invest in improvements that would ultimately be of benefit to everyone in the kingdom, such as 'policies, fair buildings, manuering of barren landis, planting of trees and fisches in fresch waters and stankes, building of Dowcattis (doocots), green orchyairdis and cunyngares (rabbit warrens)'. In turn, enriched by these investments, the occupants of the land would be able to provide themselves with 'armour and martiall furniture for defence of King and countrie againes old enemies and utheris quhatsomever that wald Invade the samen'.[114] This particular charter sett the lands of Gladswood heritably to John Robson, the sitting tenant, ostensibly in recognition of the good service that John had done for the abbey in paying towards its repair. In return for the heritable tenancy, John's annual rent increased from 26s 8d (or two merks) to 40s (three merks), plus six capons and six hens. The canons had got a 50 per cent increase in the rent, but that figure was now fixed for all time, and John Robson had been given secure and irredeemable possession of his tenancy. As inflation quickly eroded away the value of the higher rents, it soon became obvious who the beneficiaries of such deals were.

Not all of the abbey's lands, however, were disposed of at feu, and a number of traditional tenancies continued to be granted, usually in respect of smaller portions of property. One such arrangement is set out in a charter of 14 March 1554/5, given by John Erskine, commendator, to David Oswald and Alison Todryk, his wife.[115] This granted the couple two 'onsettis' (a steading with the dwelling houses and outhouses built on it) and two acres of land, one onset lying in what had been the burgh area outside the abbey precinct wall, the other in the 'west hawch' (the arable ground running north-west between the river and the hills towards Bemersyde), with grazing for two horses, four 'soums' of pasture (a reckoning based on the numbers of animals a given piece of ground could support) and the right to graze in wood and field like any other beasts of the toun of Dryburgh, plus permission to build as many houses as they pleased and various other rights. The two acres were described as 'lying in runrig throughout the field of the toun of Dryburgh', that is, it was composed of rigs or strips of ground scattered throughout the cultivated area that was worked in common by all the tenants of the toun. All of this was granted on a nineteen-year lease for an annual rent of 30s and six 'cain fowl' and six firlots of bear–barley for the two acres.

The number of feuferme grants increased steadily after the Reformation, with the Commendator, David Erskine, presiding over a systematic dismantling of the monastic estate. The Humes and the Haliburtons in Mertoun continued to be amongst the principal beneficiaries of the process. In December 1562, Andrew Hume received the feuferme of various portions of the abbey's arable lands at Dunbar for an annual rent of 30s, which represented nearly a 25 per cent drop in rental income from what had been paid by the several tenants who had occupied them previously.[116] In July 1567 Walter Haliburton, described as burgess of Dundee, had his nineteen-year lease of four merklands in Mertoun converted into a heritable tenancy paying 54s 4d and six poultry (or 4d per hen) annually.[117] The following month, Thomas Cranstoun, burgess of Lauder, and his heirs male bearing the surname Cranstoun, received a heritable tenancy of a croftland in Lauder.[118] Such piecemeal alienations seriously eroded the abbey's estate but it provided a relatively secure cash income to a lord who was rarely resident and who preferred to have his income remitted to him through his chamberlain.

By the time that David Erskine described the community as defunct in 1600, the monastic character of the estate which he then controlled had long disappeared. The precinct at its core had been converted into the mansion of a landed gentleman on one side and a series of tenanted gardens and yards occupying the ground to its west. The precinct wall had been ruptured and the lay tenants who had once been kept at arm's length beyond the abbey gates had invaded the once-forbidden inner sanctum. At a further remove, Erskine and his predecessors had progressively alienated the most significant blocks of the abbey's former estate, settling feu-charters on relatives and dependents, but breaking the old direct link between the abbey and its tenants by the heritable nature of the grants given. The change, however, should not be overstated, for like his abbatial predecessors and the canons, David's principal income source was from rents. For the majority of the former monastic tenants the question must be asked whether or not they really noticed any significant change.

Bibliography

[Abbreviations used in the notes are given in square brackets]

PRIMARY SOURCES

1. Unpublished
National Archives of Scotland
GD124: Papers of the Erskine Family, earls of Mar and Kellie.
    GD124/1/1001 Crown charter to John, earl of Mar, of all the lands which formerly pertained to the monasteries of Cambuskenneth, Dryburgh and Inchmahome.
    GD124/1/1005 Extract Act of Parliament ratifying above.
    GD124/9/14-21, 23, Bulls of Pope Paul IV granting Dryburgh to David Erskine.
GD149: Papers of the Cunninghame Family of Caprington.
    GD149/264 Royal letterbook [Caprington Letterbook]
GD259: Papers of the Scott family of Ancrum
    GD259/4/23 Bundle of miscellaneous writs and inventories, 1486-1813.

2. Published
Acts of the Parliaments of Scotland, ed. T. Thomson and C. Innes (Edinburgh, 1814-75) [*Acts Parl. Scot.*]
Calendar of Documents Relating to Scotland, ed. J. Bain (Edinburgh, 1881-8) [*CDS*]
Calendar of Scottish Supplications to Rome, 1418-22, ed. E.R. Lindsay and A.I. Cameron (Scottish History Society, 1934) [*CSSR 1418-22*]
Calendar of Scottish Supplications to Rome, 1428-33, ed. I.B. Cowan and A.I. Dunlop (Scottish History Society, 1970) [*CSSR 1428-33*]
Calendar of State Papers Relating to Scotland, i, *1509-1589,* ed. M.J. Thorpe (London, 1858) [*Cal. State Papers Scot.*]
Charters of David I, ed. G.W.S. Barrow (Woodbridge, 1999) [*Charters of David I*]
Chronicle of Melrose, ed. A.O. Anderson et al. (London, 1936) [*Chron. Melrose*]
Chronici Henrici Knighton, ed. J.R. Lumby, 2 vols, (Rolls Series, London, 1889-95) [*Chron. Henrici Knighton*]
English Historical Documents, iii, ed. H. Rothwell (London, 1975) [*Eng. Hist. Docs*]
Exchequer Rolls of Scotland, ed. J. Stuart et al. (Edinburgh 1878-1908) [*Exch. Rolls*]
Historical Manuscripts Commission, 11th Report, Appendix Part VI. The Manuscripts of the Duke of Hamilton, KT (London, 1887) [*Hamilton Manuscripts*]
John Barbour, *The Bruce,* ed. A.A.M. Duncan (Edinburgh, 1997) [Barbour, *The Bruce*]
The Letters of James V, ed. R.K. Hannay and D. Hay (Edinburgh, 1954) [*James V Letters*]
Liber Sancte Marie de Calchou (Bannatyne Club, 1846) [*Kel. Liber*]

Dryburgh Abbey

Liber Sancte Marie de Dryburgh (Bannatyne Club, 1847) [*Dryburgh Liber*]
Liber Sancte Marie de Melros (Bannatyne Club, 1837) [*Mel. Liber*]
Regesta Regum Scotorum, i, *the Acts of Malcolm IV*, ed. G.W.S. Barrow (Edinburgh, 1960) [*RRS*, i]
Regesta Regum Scotorum, ii, *the Acts of William I*, ed. G.W.S. Barrow (Edinburgh, 1971) [*RRS*, ii]
Regesta Regum Scotorum, v, *the Acts of Robert I*, ed. A.A.M. Duncan (Edinburgh, 1988) [*RRS*, v]
Regesta Regum Scotorum, vi, *the Acts of David II*, ed. B. Webster (Edinburgh, 1976) [*RRS*, vi]
The Register and Records of Holm Cultram, ed. F. Grainger and W.G. Collingwood (Cumberland and
    Westmorland Antiquarian and Archaeological Society, 1929) [*Register of Holm Cultram*]
The Register of the Priory of St Bees, ed. J. Wilson (Surtees Society, 1915) [*Register of St Bees*]
Registrum Magni Sigilii Regum Scotorum, ed. J.M. Thomson et al. (Edinburgh 1882-1914) [*RMS*]
Registrum Secreti Sigilii Regum Scotorum, ed. M. Livingstone et al. (Edinburgh 1908-) [*RSS*]
Rotuli Scotiae in Turri Londiniensi et in Domo Capitulari Westmonasteriensi Asservati, ed D. Macpherson et
    al., 2 vols (London, 1814-19) [*Rotuli Scotiae*]
Walter Bower, *Scotichronicon*, ed. D.E.R. Watt et al., 9 vols (Aberdeen and Edinburgh, 1987-97)
    [Bower, *Scotichronicon*]
Wigtownshire Charters, ed. R.C. Reid (Scottish History Society, 1960) [*Wigtownshire Charters*]

SECONDARY WORKS

1. Books
Backmund, N., *Monasticon Praemonstratense*, ii (Staubing, 1952) [*Monasticon Praemonstratense*]
Brooke, D., *Wild Men and Holy Places* (Edinburgh, 1994) [Brooke, *Wild Men and Holy Places*]
Brown, M., *The Black Douglases* (East Linton, 1998) [Brown, *Black Douglases*]
Bulloch, J., *Adam of Dryburgh* (London, 1958) [Bulloch, *Adam of Dryburgh*]
Cowan, I.B., *The Parishes of Medieval Scotland* (Scottish Record Society, 1967) [Cowan, *Parishes*]
Cowan, I.B., *Ayrshire Abbeys: Crossraguel and Kilwinning* (Ayrshire Archaeological and Natural History
    Society, 1986) [Cowan, *Crossraguel and Kilwinning*]
Cowan, I.B., and Easson, D.E., *Medieval Relgious Houses, Scotland* (2nd ed., London and New York,
    1976) [Cowan and Easson, *Religious Houses*]
Cruft, K., Dunbar, J., and Fawcett, R., *The Buildings of Scotland, Borders* (New Haven and London,
    2005).
Duncan, A.A.M., *Scotland: the Making of the Kingdom* (Edinburgh, 1978) [Duncan, *Making of the
    Kingdom*]
Easson, D.E., *Medieval Religious Houses, Scotland* (London, 1957) [Easson, *Religious Houses*]
Fawcett, R., *Scottish Abbeys and Priories* (London, 1994)
Fawcett, R., *Scottish Medieval Churches, Architecture and Furnishings* (Stroud, 2002) [Fawcett, *Medieval
    Churches*]
Fawcett, R. and Oram, R, *Melrose Abbey* (Stroud, 2004) [Fawcett and Oram, *Melrose*]
Ferguson, P.C., *Medieval Papal Representatives in Scotland: Legates, Nuncios, and Judges Delegate, 1125-1286*
    (Stair Society, 1997) [Ferguson, *Papal Representatives*]
Gribbin, J.A., *The Premonstratensian Order in Late Medieval England* (Woodbridge, 2001) [Gribbin,
    Premonstratensian Order]
Hartridge, R.A.R., *A History of Vicarages in the Middle Ages* (Cambridge, 1930) [Hartridge, *Vicarages*]
Hogg, J., *The Scottish Border Abbeys*, i (Analecta Cartusiana, xxxv, Salzburg, 1986) [Hogg, *Border Abbeys*]
MacGibbon, D., and Ross, T., *The Ecclesiastical Architecture of Scotland*, 3 vols (Edinburgh, 1896-7)
    [MacGibbon and Ross, *Ecclesiastical Architecture*]
McNeill, T.E., *Anglo-Norman Ulster: the History and Archaeology of an Irish Barony, 1177-1400* (Edinburgh,
    1980) [McNeill, *Anglo-Norman Ulster*]
Manuel, D.G., *Dryburgh Abbey in the Light of its Historical and Ecclesiastical Setting* (Edinburgh, 1992)
Midmer, R., *English Medieval Monasteries* (London, 1979) [Midmer, *Monasteries*]
Nicholson, R., *Scotland: the Later Middle Ages* (Edinburgh, 1974) [Nicholson, *Later Middle Ages*]

Oram, R.D., *The Lordship of Galloway* (Edinburgh, 2000) [Oram, *Lordship of Galloway*]

Oram, R.D., *David I: the King who made Scotland* (Stroud, 2004) [Oram, *David I*]

Richardson, J.S. and Wood, M., *Dryburgh Abbey, Berwickshire* (official guidebook, 1948) [Richardson and Wood, *Dryburgh Abbey*]

Royal Commission on the Ancient and Historical Monuments of Scotland, *Inventory of Berwickshire* (2nd ed., Edinburgh, 1915) [RCAHMS, *Berwickshire*]

Watt, D.E.R. and Shead, N.F., (eds), *The Heads of Religious Houses in Scotland from Twelfth to Sixteenth Centuries* (Scottish Record Society, 2001) [Watt and Shead, *Heads of religious Houses*]

2. Articles

Backmund, N., 'The Premonstratensian Order in Scotland', *Innes Review*, 4 (1952-3), 25-41 [Backmund, 'Premonstratensian Order in Scotland']

Cowan, I.B., 'Some aspects of the appropriation of parish churches in medieval Scotland', *Records of the Scottish Church History Society*, 13 (1957-9), 202-222 [Cowan, 'Appropriation']

Duffy, S., 'The first Ulster plantation: John de Courcy and the men of Cumbria', in T. Barry, R. Frame and K. Simms, *Colony and Frontier in Medieval Ireland: essays presented to J.F. Lydon* (London, 1995), 1-27 [Duffy, 'Ulster plantation']

McDonald, R.A., 'Scoto-Norse kings and the reformed religious orders: patterns of monastic patronage in twelfth-century Galloway and Argyll', *Albion*, 27 (1995) [McDonald, 'Scoto-Norse kings']

Macfarlane, L.J., 'The primacy of the Scottish Church, 1472-1521', *Innes Review*, 20 (1969), 111-129 [Macfarlane, 'Primacy']

Oram, R.D., 'Dervorgilla, the Balliols and Buittle', *Transactions of the Dumfriesshire and Galloway Natural History and Antiquarian Society*, 73 (1999), 165-181 [Oram, 'Dervorgilla']

Simpson, G.G. and Webster, B. 'Charter evidence and the distribution of mottes in Scotland', in K.J. Stringer (ed.), *Essays on the Nobility of Medieval Scotland* (Edinburgh, 1985), 1-24 [Simpson and Webster, 'Charter evidence']

Stringer, K.J., 'The early lords of Lauderdale, Dryburgh Abbey and St Andrews Priory at Northhampton', in K.J. Stringer (ed.), *Essays on the Nobility of Medieval Scotland* (Edinburgh, 1985), 44-71 [Stringer, 'Early lords']

Stringer, K.J., 'Nobility and identity in medieval Britain and Ireland: the de Vescy family, c.1120-1314', in B. Smith (ed.), *Britain and Ireland 900-1300: Insular Responses to Medieval European Change* (Cambridge, 1999), 199-239 [Stringer, 'Nobility and identity']

Notes

CHAPTER 1: THE HISTORY OF THE ABBEY

1 This was published in the nineteenth century as the *Liber Sancte Marie de Dryburgh* (Bannatyne Club, 1847).

2 *Charters of David I*, no. 202 and note.

3 *Chron. Melrose*, s.a. 1162.

4 *Dryburgh Liber*, iii, v-vi.

5 For Beatrice's gifts to the abbey, see *Charters of David I*, nos 192, 202; *Dryburgh Liber*, nos 14, 15, 93, 145, 239, 240.

6 Oram, *David I*, 116, 117, 119, 126-127, 143, 173, 180.

7 C. Brooke, *The Age of the Cloister: the Story of Monastic Life in the Middle Ages* (Stroud, 2003), 217-219; Backmund, 'Premonstratensian Order in Scotland', 25-41 at 25-27.

8 Backmund, 'Premonstratensian Order in Scotland', 26.

9 Midmer, *Monasteries*, 232. It was colonised from Licques Abbey near Boulogne, a daughter-house of Prémontré.

10 *Chron. Melrose*, s.a. 1148; Midmer, *Monasteries*, 49-50

11 Stringer, 'Nobility and identity', 199-239 at 223-224 and note 115.

12 *Chron. Melrose*, s.a. 1150.

13 *Chron. Melrose*, s.a. 1152.

14 *Dryburgh Liber*, nos 239, 240, 241, 249. See *RRS*, i, no. 172 and *RRS*, ii, no. 65 for comment on the dating and content of the charters of Malcolm IV and William.

15 *Dryburgh Liber*, no. 147.

16 For example, *Dryburgh Liber*, no. 201.

17 Stringer, 'Early lords', 45; *Dryburgh Liber*, no. 93.

18 *Dryburgh Liber*, nos 143-145, 147.

19 *Chron. Melrose*, s.a. 1162; *RRS*, i, 34-5. His status as founder of Dryburgh is recorded in his obituary in the Chronicle. For 'the day on which Hugh de Morville assumed canonical habit', see *Dryburgh Liber*, no. 8.

20 Easson, *Religious Houses,* 149. For the foundation charter of the hospital, see *Dryburgh Liber*, appendix, no. 1.

21 Watt and Shead, *Heads of Religious Houses*, 127.

22 Cowan, *Crossraguel and Kilwinning*, 268-270.

23 *Dryburgh Liber*, nos 84-87; Ferguson, *Papal Representatives*, 233.

24 *Chron. Melrose*, s.a. 1177; Watt and Shead, *Heads of Religious Houses*, 58.

25 Watt and Shead, *Heads of Religious Houses*, 58.

26 Backmund, 'Premonstratensian Order in Scotland', 34.

27 For a brief outline of some of his ideas, see Duncan*, Making of the Kingdom*, 456-457. His life and work is studied in detail in Bulloch, *Adam of Dryburgh*.

28 Richardson and Wood, *Dryburgh Abbey*, 15, 17.

29 *Monasticon Praemonstratense*, ii. [On-line at: http://www.premontre.org/subpages/loci/monasticon/circariae/2hib.htm]; McNeill, *Anglo-Norman Ulster*, 14.

30 Duffy, 'Ulster plantation', 1-27; Oram, *Lordship of Galloway*, 195-6.

31 Ferguson, *Papal Representatives*, 86-87; *Dryburgh Liber*, nos 23, 26, 27, 35, 36, 101, 234.

32 *Chron. Melrose*, s.a. 1240.

33 *Dryburgh Liber*, no. 38.

34 *Calendar of Entries in the Papal Registers relating to Great Britain and Ireland: Papal Letters*, ed. W.H. Bliss et al. (London 1893-), i, p 309.

35 *Dryburgh Liber*, no. 256.

36 *Dryburgh Liber*, nos 260 and 274.

37 *Dryburgh Liber*, no. 119.

38 *Dryburgh Liber*, no. 120.

39 *Dryburgh Liber*, no. 174.

40 *Dryburgh Liber*, no. 204.

41 For the patronage of the lords of Galloway, see Brooke, *Wild Men and Holy Places*, 88-90, 104-106, 124-126, 140-149; McDonald, 'Scoto-Norse kings'.

42 *Wigtownshire Charters*, no. 129; *Kel. Liber*, no.468; *Register of Holm Cultram*, nos 120, 121; *Register of St Bees*, no. 62.

43 *Dryburgh Liber*, nos 138-141.

44 Oram, *Lordship of Galloway*, 148-149, 159; Oram, 'Dervorgilla', 165-181 at 169, 174.

45 *CDS*, ii, no. 189.

46 *CDS*, ii, no. 817.

47 *Rotuli Scotiae in Turri Londiniensi et in Domo Capitulari Westmonasteriensi Asservati*, ed. D. Macpherson et al, 2 vols (London, 1814-19), i, 24b.

48 *CDS*, iii, no. 163

49 *CDS*, iii, no. 509.

50 *RRS*, v, no. 100.

51 Barbour, *The Bruce*, 685.

52 Bower, *Scotichronicon*, vii, 11-13.

53 *RRS*, v, no. 283 and note; *Dryburgh Liber*, nos 305, 306.

54 For his contrasting behaviour elsewhere, see Fawcett and Oram, *Melrose Abbey*, 38-39.

55 *Dryburgh Liber*, no. 296.

56 *Dryburgh Liber*, no. 297.

57 *Dryburgh Liber*, no. 299.

58 *Dryburgh Liber*, no. 307.

59 *Dryburgh Liber*, nos 300-304, 308-312.

60 *Dryburgh Liber*, nos 313-316.

61 *CDS*, iii, no. 1185.

62 Nicholson, *Later Middle Ages*, 131-132.

63 *RRS*, vi, no. 89; *Dryburgh Liber*, appendix, docs iii-v.

64 *Rotuli Scotiae*, i, 788a.

65 *Mel. Liber*, ii, no.433.

66 *Rotuli Scotiae*, i, 958a.

67 Bower, *Scotichronicon*, vii, 407.

68 *Chron. Henrici Knighton*, 204-205.

69 *RMS*, i, no. 832. Traill, Fife and Douglas all witnessed the charter.

70 The 1391 grant marked the start of a protracted exercise before the canons finally gained undisputed possession of the nunnery's lands, with a succession of appeals and counter-appeals by would-be prioresses of the house and the canons and their supporters (*CSSR, 1418-1422*, 152-153 [22 January 1420], 196-197 [13 May 1420]; *CSSR, 1428-1432*, 30-31 [31 July 1429], 66-68 [30 December 1429]; 243-244 [7 August 1432]). As late as November 1464, the government of the young King James III was issuing confirmations of Robert III's grant (*RMS*, ii, no. 820).

71 *Brown, Black Douglases*, 185-187.

72 *CSSR, 1418-1422*, 197.

73 *CSSR, 1428-32*, 66-68.

74 *CSSR, 1428-32*, 255.

75 *CSSR, 1428-1432*, 163-164.

76 Bower, *Scotichronicon*, vii, 175.

77 Registra Supplicationum in Vat. Arch. (Manuscript calendar of entries held by the Department of Scottish History, University of Glasgow), 542, fol 255.

78 Watt and Shead, *Heads of Religious Houses*, 60.

79 *Dryburgh Liber*, appendix, doc. xiii.

80 *Dryburgh Liber*, xvii-xviii.

81 *Dryburgh Liber*, xvi. The name seems to have been applied to the Lanarkshire group of properties by the fifteenth century: see, for example *Dryburgh Liber*, no. 47, where the lands are referred to as 'the grange of Ingbuston'.

82 *Dryburgh Liber*, xvi-xvii.

83 Watt and Shead. *Heads of Religious Houses*, 60

84 For detail of the foregoing, see Watt and Shead, *Heads of Religious Houses*, 60-61.

85 For a discussion of this dispute, see Backmund, 'Premonstratensian Order in Scotland', 31-32.

86 Watt and Shead, *Heads of Religious Houses*, 61.

87 Nicholson, *Later Middle Ages*, 559-560.

88 Watt and Shead, *Heads of Religious Houses*, 52.

89 Watt and Shead, *Heads of Religious Houses*, 147.

90 Watt and Shead, *Heads of Religious Houses*, 125.

91 Watt and Shead, *Heads of Religious Houses*, 8.

92 *James V Letters*, 30.

93 For a detailed discussion of Forman's career and contribution to Scottish religious life, see Macfarlane, 'Primacy', 111-129.

94 Watt and Shead, *Heads of Religious Houses*, 61.

95 *RSS*, i, no. 2796.

96 *James V Letters*, 61-62.

97 For the Glenluce dispute, see *Wigtownshire Charters*, 60, 61.

98 *Hamilton Manuscripts*, no. 66.

99 *James V Letters*, 95.

100 *Cal. State Papers Scot.*, i, *1509-1589*, 16.

101 For this relationship, see *Dryburgh Liber*, Appendix, doc. xxiii.

102 NAS GD 259/4/23.

103 NAS GD 149/264/folio 45; *RMS*, iii, no. 2332; *Dryburgh Liber*, appendix, doc. xviii.

104 Watt and Shead, *Heads of Religious Houses*, 61.

105 *James V Letters*, 286.

106 *James V Letters*, 380.

107 Watt and Shead, *Heads of Religious Houses*, 61-62.

108 Fawcett and Oram, *Melrose Abbey*, 59-60.

109 *Letters and Papers, Foreign and Domestic of the Reign of Henry VIII*, J.S. Brewer et al (ed.), xix[2], no. 625

110 *Cal. State Papers Scot.*, i, 56.

111 *Dryburgh Liber*, xxiv.

112 *Cal. State Papers Scot.*, i, no. 9.

113 *Cal. State Papers Scot.*, i, no. 15.

114 *Cal. State Papers Scot.*, i, nos 18 and 1180.

115 *Cal. State Papers Scot.*, i, no. 101.

116 Watt and Shead, *Heads of Religious Houses*, 61-62.

117 Watt and Shead, *Heads of Religious Houses*, 62. NAS GD124/9/14-21, 23.

118 *Dryburgh Liber*, Appendix, pt iii, no. xlvii.

119 *Dryburgh Liber*, Appendix, pt iii, no. xlvii, 403.

120 *Dryburgh Liber*, xxvii.

121 *Acts Parl. Scot.*, iii, 335, 381; *RMS*, v, no. 723.

122 *RMS*, v, no.723; Watt and Shead, *Heads of Religious Houses*, 62.

123 *Dryburgh Liber*, appendix, nos xv and xvi.

124 *Dryburgh Liber*, appendix, nos xviii-xx.

125 *Dryburgh Liber*, appendix, nos xxi-xxiii.

126 *Dryburgh Liber*, appendix, pt iii, no. xlvii, 401.

127 *Dryburgh Liber*, appendix, nos xxvi-xxxii.

128 *Dryburgh Liber*, appendix, no.xxxiii.

129 NAS GD124/1/1001; *Acts Parl. Scot.*, iv, 343-348.

130 Watt and Shead, *Heads of Religious Houses*, 62.

CHAPTER 2: THE ARCHITECTURE OF THE ABBEY

1 Summary accounts of the foundation of the Scottish Premonstratensian houses will be found in Cowan and Easson, *Religious Houses, Scotland* , 100-104.

2 The architecture of Dryburgh Abbey has been very inadequately studied and published, the main accounts in print being: MacGibbon and Ross, *Ecclesiastical Architecture*, i, 448-464; RCAHMS, *Berwickshire* 132-148; Richardson and Wood, *Dryburgh Abbey*; Hogg, *Border Abbeys*, i, 87-127.

3 A.G. MacGregor and R.J.A. Eckford, 'The stones of the abbeys of the Scottish Borders', *Transactions of the Edinburgh Geological Society*, 14 (1952), 246-248.

4 K.A. Steer and J.W.M. Bannerman, *Late Medieval Monumental Sculpture in the Western Highlands* (Edinburgh, 1977), 5.

5 J.A. Smith, 'Notice of an incised slab found some years ago near Newstead, Roxburghshire', *Proceedings of the Society of Antiquaries of Scotland*, 1 (1851-4), 229-230.

6 Alnwick was founded by Eustace FitzJohn in 1147. (D. Knowles and R.N. Hadcock, *Medieval religious houses, England and Wales* (2nd ed, London, 1971), 185.)

7 For a brief account of the excavation of Alnwick Abbey, see W.H. St John Hope, 'On the Premonstratensian abbey of St Mary at Alnwick, Northumberland', *Archaeological Journal*, 44 (1887), 337-346.

8 For a discussion of the Premonstratensian liturgy, see Gribbin, *Premonstratensian Order*, 101-131.

9 For a brief discussion of the furnishings that might be found see Fawcett, *Medieval Churches*.

10 R. Gilyard-Beer and G. Coppack, 'Excavations at Fountains Abbey, 1979-80', *Archeologia*, 108 (1986), 147-188; G. Coppack, C. Hayfield and R. Williams. 'Sawley Abbey: the architecture and archaeology of a smaller Cistercian abbey', *Journal of the British Archaeological Association*, 155 (2002), 22-114; G. Coppack, '"According to the form of the order": the earliest Cistercian buildings in England and their context', in T. N. Kinder (ed.), *Perspectives for an Architecture of Solitude* (Turnhout, 2004), 35-45.

11 There is a fragment of what looks to be a chamfered base course at the west end of the south side of the presbytery, where it meets the choir aisle. However, it is very difficult to interpret this stone, and it may be no more than a fragment that was placed there as part of the consolidation of the wall core.

12 M. Thurlby, 'Glasgow Cathedral and the wooden barrel vault in twelfth- and thirteenth-century architecture in Scotland', in R Fawcett (ed.), *Medieval Art and Architecture in the Diocese of Glasgow* (British Archaeological Association Conference Transactions, Leeds, 1998), 84-87.

13 For discussion of the dating of Elgin see R. Fawcett, *Elgin Cathedral* (Edinburgh, 2001).

14 At Glasgow rebuilding was probably in progress on the eastern limb when funds were being sought in 1242; a dendrochronological date of *c.*1258 has been established for ex-situ roof timbers. For discussion of the dating of Glasgow see R. Fawcett, 'Glasgow Cathedral', in E. Williamson, A. Riches and M. Higgs, *The Buildings of Scotland, Glasgow* (London, 1990), 108-135.

15 See previous note for the dating of Glasgow; at Inchmahome the priory was founded *c.*1238, and building was probably in progress soon afterwards. (See R. Fawcett, *Inchmahome Priory* (official guidebook, Edinburgh, 1986).)

16 Tintern was rebuilt from 1269 to 1301. (See D.M. Robinson, *Tintern Abbey* (official guidebook, 3rd ed. Cardiff, 1995).)

17 General rebuilding of Westminster was started on the orders of Henry III in 1245. (See P. Binski, *Westminster Abbey and the Plantagenets* (New Haven and London, 1995).)

18 See N. Pevsner, *The Buildings of England, Staffordshire* (Harmondsworth, 1974), 179-183.

19 The north transept at Hereford was built by Bishop Aquablanca (1240-68). (See N. Pevsner, *The Buildings of England, Herefordshire* (Harmondsworth, 1963), 158-159.)

20 V. Jansen, 'Dying mouldings, unarticulated springer blocks and hollow chamfers in thirteenth-century architecture, *Journal of the British Archaeological Association*, 135 (1982), 35-54.

21 See Fawcett, *op. cit.* note 13, 42-43.

22 For discussion of the dating of Pluscarden see R. Fawcett, 'The priory church', in F. McCormick et al., 'Excavations at Pluscarden Priory, Moray', *Proceedings of the Society of Antiquaries of Scotland*, 124 (1994), 396-403.

23 For measured drawings of Sweetheart see *The Five Great Churches of Galloway* (Ayrshire and Galloway Archaeological Association, Edinburgh, 1899), 1-55.

24 See R. Fawcett, 'Culross Abbey', in Kinder, *op. cit.* note 10, 81-99.

25 See Fawcett, *Medieval Churches*, fig. 2.84 (8).

26 See Fawcett, *Medieval Churches*, fig. 3.27 (12).

27 Talley was founded by Rhys ap Gruffudd between 1184 and 1189. (See D.M. Robinson and C. Platt, *Strata Florida Abbey; Talley Abbey* (official guidebook, rev. ed., Cardiff, 1998).)

28 E. Fernie, *The Architecture of Norman England* (Oxford, 2000), 289.

29 G.S.B. Prospection Ltd, *Geophysical survey report 2004/59, Dryburgh Abbey* (Bradford, 2004).

30 Hector Boece said that greater ceremony in the liturgy reached Scotland in the reign of James I (1406-37). (*Scotorum Historia* (2nd ed, Paris, 1574) fols 348-349.)

31 See Fawcett Fawcett, *Medieval Churches*, fig. 2.84 (14).

32 The Jedburgh north transept has the arms of Bishop Turnbull of Glasgow (1447-54).

33 See R. Fawcett, 'Reliving bygone glories?: the revival of earlier architectural forms in Scottish late medieval church architecture', *Journal of the British Archaeological Association*, 156 (2003), 104-137

34 See Fawcett, *Medieval Churches*, figs 3.11 (2) and (3).

35 This base appears to be from a pier of four shafts, and could have come from a corner of the cloister.

36 See W.H. St John Hope, 'Fountains Abbey, Yorkshire', *Yorkshire Archaeological Journal*, 15 (1898-99), fig. 12.

37 P. Ferguson, *Architecture of Solitude* (Princeton, 1984), figs 113 and 115.

38 See F. Bond, *The Chancel of English Churches* (Oxford, 1916), 156.

39 See Fawcett, *Medieval Churches*, figs 3.78, 3.79 and 3.82.

40 A study of the painted decoration was carried out by Historic Scotland's Conservation Centre, *Dryburgh Abbey – Chapter House Conservation Report* (Edinburgh, 2003).

41 W.H. St John Hope, *op. cit.* note 36, 103-115.

42 J. Newman, *The Buildings of Wales, Glamorgan* (London, 1995), 421 and 426-427.

43 Robert I gave funds to the Dunfermline refectory shortly before his death in 1329 (*Exch. Rolls*, i, 215).

44 This phase of work at Mugdock is generally thought to have been instigated by Sir David de Graham, who died *c.*1376, see Royal Commission on the Ancient and Historical Monuments of Scotland, *Inventory of Stirlingshire* (Edinburgh, 1963), i, 253 and pl. 109A.

45 RCAHMS, *Berwickshire*, fig. 129.

46 See R. Fawcett, D. McRoberts and F. Stewart, *Inchcolm Abbey and Island* (official guidebook, Edinburgh, 1998), 13.

47 D. Knowles, *The Religious Orders in England*, ii (Cambridge, 1955), 139.

48 For a brief account of the Buchan's life see R.G. Cant, 'David Steuart Erskine, 11th earl of Buchan, founder of the Society of Antiquaries of Scotland', in A.S. Bell (ed.) *The Scottish Antiquarian Tradition* (Edinburgh, 1981), 1-30.

49 F. Grose, *The Antiquities of Scotland*, ii (London, 1789), 101-109.

50 *The Statistical Account of Scotland*, ed. J. Sinclair, xiv (Edinburgh, 1795), 592.

51 A.A. Tait, *The Landscape Garden in Scotland* (Edinburgh, 1980) 201.

CHAPTER 3: THE ESTATES AND POSSESSIONS OF THE ABBEY

1 *Dryburgh Liber*, nos 239, 240.

2 Fawcett and Oram, *Melrose Abbey*, 212–213.

3 *Dryburgh Liber*, no. 161.

4 *Dryburgh Liber*, no. 241.

5 *Dryburgh Liber*, no. 58 takes an 'ancient' or 'old' ditch as one of the boundary lines of a portion of property granted the parish church of Lessudden (St Boswell's) by Thomas of London in *c.*1153; *ibid.*, no. 110, refers to an 'ancient structure' or 'work' as a boundary point of an assart (clearance for agriculture from the woodland or grassland) beside Kedslie on the west side of the Leader in the later 1100s; and *ibid.*, no. 114 also has an 'ancient ditch' providing a boundary between the earl of Dunbar's property of Earlston in Lauderdale and the canons' grange at Kedslie.

6 *Dryburgh Liber*, no. 109.

7 *Dryburgh Liber*, no. 109

8 *Dryburgh Liber*, no. 147.

9 *Dryburgh Liber*, no. 110.

10 *Dryburgh Liber*, no. 109.

11 *RRS*, i, no. 235 confirmed Melrose's interests in the uplands around the valley of the Allan Water, immediately west of Kedslie. *RRS*, ii, no. 236, dated 1178x1188, settled a long-running dispute with Richard de Morville, which conceded extensive grazing rights to the monks in the forest areas around Colmslie, Threepwood and Buckholm.

12 *Dryburgh Liber*, nos 112 and 240, which confirm the canons' rights to pasture in the forest area.

13 *Dryburgh Liber*, no. 113.

14 *RRS*, i, no. 235.

15 *RRS*, ii, no. 236.

16 *Dryburgh Liber*, no. 176.

17 *Dryburgh Liber*, nos 181–186.

18 *Dryburgh Liber*, no. 16.

19 *Dryburgh Liber*, no. 161.

20 See *Dryburgh Liber*, no. 22 for confirmation of the grant by Henry of Anstruther and no. 251 for confirmation of possession in a papal bull of Pope Gregory IX, dated June 1228.

21 *Dryburgh Liber*, nos 302, 303.

22 *Dryburgh Liber*, no. 7.

23 *Dryburgh Liber*, nos 188–191.

24 *Dryburgh Liber*, nos 301, 304

25 *Dryburgh Liber*, no. 104.

26 Simpson and Webster, 'Charter evidence', 1–24 at 2–5

27 For this land, the tenant, Reginald Tayllur, and his heirs would pay the canons annually at Witsunday rent of one stone of beeswax.

28 *Dryburgh Liber*, no. 23. This is incorrectly dated in the Bannatyne Club edition to *c.*1170, despite its internal dating given by the presence of Master James the penitentiary and papal chaplain, papal legate to Scotland in 1221.

29 *Dryburgh Liber*, nos 25 and 26.

30 *Dryburgh Liber*, no. 42.

31 *Dryburgh Liber*, nos 43, 46–48, 209, 211, 217–219.

32 *Dryburgh Liber*, no. 300.

33 *Dryburgh Liber*, no. 310.

34 *Dryburgh Liber*, no. 124.

35 *Dryburgh Liber*, no. 162.

36 Duncan, *Making of the Kingdom*, 429–431

37 *Dryburgh Liber*, no. 250.

38 Fawcett and Oram, *Melrose Abbey*, 243–4; *Kelso Liber*, no. 254.

39 *Dryburgh Liber*, nos 177, 178.

40 *Dryburgh Liber*, nos 205, 206.

41 *Dryburgh Liber*, no. 226.

42 *Dryburgh Liber*, no. 133.

43 *Dryburgh Liber*, no. 255.

44 *Dryburgh Liber*, nos 143 and 147.

45 *Dryburgh Liber*, nos 143 and 147.

46 *Dryburgh Liber*, nos 146 and 147.

47 *Dryburgh Liber*, no. 148.

48 *Dryburgh Liber*, nos 307, 313-316.

49 *Dryburgh Liber*, nos 214 and 215.

50 Fawcett and Oram, *Melrose Abbey*, 246-249, 263-266.

51 *Dryburgh Liber*, no. 154.

52 *Dryburgh Liber*, no. 143.

53 *Dryburgh Liber*, nos 92 and 129.

54 *Dryburgh Liber*, no. 132.

55 *Dryburgh Liber*, no. 42.

56 *Dryburgh Liber*, no. 175.

57 *Dryburgh Liber*, no. 237.

58 *Dryburgh Liber*, no. 312.

59 Cowan, *Parishes*, 216.

60 See *Dryburgh Liber*, no. 249.

61 *Dryburgh Liber*, no. 279.

62 *Eng. His. Docs*, iii, 643-76 at 658-59; Canon 32 of the decrees of the Fourth Lateran Council, cited in Hartridge, *Vicarages*, 20-21. For a discussion of the problem, see Cowan, 'Appropriation', 202-222.

63 *Dryburgh Liber*, no. 237.

64 *Dryburgh Liber*, nos 10 and 40; Cowan, *Parishes*, 30.

65 *Dryburgh Liber*, nos 186 and 191.

66 *Dryburgh Liber*, nos 29-32.

67 *Dryburgh Liber*, nos 265, 266; Ferguson, *Papal Representatives*, 233.

68 *Dryburgh Liber*, no. 279.

69 *Dryburgh Liber*, no. 12. Cowan, *Parishes*, 129 gives only two chaplains. By 1318 the canons were obliged only to pay for one chaplain at Lauder (*Dryburgh Liber*, no. 293).

70 *Dryburgh Liber*, no. 23. This is incorrectly dated in the Bannatyne Club edition to *c.*1170, despite its internal dating given by the presence of Master James the penitentiary and papal chaplain, papal legate to Scotland in 1221.

71 *Dryburgh Liber*, nos 25, 26, 35-37.

72 *Dryburgh Liber*, no. 27.

73 *Dryburgh Liber*, nos 16 (Confirmation by Countess Ada of an earlier grant), 253.

74 *Dryburgh Liber*, nos 18, 234, 237, 262.

75 *Dryburgh Liber*, no. 40.

76 *Dryburgh Liber*, no. 98.

77 Cowan, *Parishes*, 7.

78 *Dryburgh Liber*, no. 192.

79 The whole relationship of Dryburgh with Bozeat is analysed in detail in Stringer, 'Early lords', 44-71.

80 *Dryburgh Liber*, no. 93.

81 *RRS*, i, 10.

82 Stringer, 'Early lords', 53 and appendix, doc. 1.

83 Stringer, 'Early lords', appendix doc. 2.

84 *Dryburgh Liber*, nos 94, 95, 97; Stringer, 'Early lords', 54-55 and appendix doc. 4.

85 Stringer, 'Early lords', appendix docs 4 and 5.

86 Stringer, 'Early lords', 45-46 and appendix docs 6-8.

87 Stringer, 'Early lords', 55 and appendix docs 9-11.

88 *Dryburgh Liber*, no. 68.

89 Oram, *Lordship of Galloway*, 195-6.

90 *Dryburgh Liber*, no. 64; Cowan, *Parishes*, 20.

91 *Dryburgh Liber*, nos 66, 67, 69, 70.

92 *CSSR, 1423-1428*, 170.

93 *Dryburgh Liber*, nos 75-79.

94 *Dryburgh Liber*, nos 71-74.

95 Robert de Vieuxpont, certainly, had given additional landed endowments to Lesser Sorbie (*Dryburgh Liber*, no. 73).

96 *Dryburgh Liber*, no. 82.

97 *Dryburgh Liber*, no. 283.

98 *Dryburgh Liber*, appendix, no. xli, Rental of Dryburgh *c.*1555, 350; *ibid.*, appendix, no. xliii, Rentale de Dryburgh *c.*1560-70, 357.

99 *Dryburgh Liber*, nos 43 and 46.

100 *Dryburgh Liber*, no. 45.

101 *Dryburgh Liber*, nos 211-219.

102 *Dryburgh Liber*, no. 296 and appendix, docs ii and iii.

103 *Dryburgh Liber*, no. 23. In *c.*1300, Alexander de Vaux, lord of Dirleton, referred to two canons serving in the chantry on the island, which he had permitted them to abandon 'in view of the imminent danger of the times'. One was to serve instead in the chapel of Stodfald, the other to celebrate at an altar in Dryburgh (*Dryburgh Liber*, no. 289).

104 *RMS*, iii, no. 430.

105 *RMS*, v, no. 173.

106 These three canons survived into the later 1580s or 1590s, but were described as all dead before 1600 (see above p.37).

107 *RMS*, v, no. 796.

108 *Dryburgh Liber*, appendix, no. xiii.

109 *Dryburgh Liber*, nos 155, 157, 254, 299.

110 *RMS*, iii, no. 2332.

111 *Dryburgh Liber*, appendix, no. xiv.

112 *Dryburgh Liber*, appendix, no. xv.

113 *Dryburgh Liber*, appendix, no. xvii.

114 *Dryburgh Liber*, appendix, no. vi.

115 *Dryburgh Liber*, appendix, no. xix.

116 *RMS*, iv, no. 2630, royal confirmation dated 16 January 1577 of the original charter dated 18 December 1562.

117 *RMS*, iv, no. 1882, royal confirmation of 2 September 1569 of the original charter of 17 July 1567.

118 *RMS*, iv, no. 2034, royal confirmation dated 18 March 1572 of the original charter dated 15 August 1567.

Index

If you are interested in purchasing other books published by Tempus,
or in case you have difficulty finding any Tempus books in your local bookshop,
you can also place orders directly through our website

www.tempus-publishing.com